What my Sherpa taught me about TEAMS

A guide to **engagement** at work

Jade Lee

PRAISE FOR *WHAT MY SHERPA TAUGHT ME ABOUT TEAMS*

'Leadership is more than the destination; it's always about how we journey together. In this lovely, well-researched book, Jade Lee shares poignant personal insights on how we might achieve the humility and care embodied in some of the most remarkable humans, Sherpas.'

Zoë Routh – Leadership Expert and author of 2020 Business Book of the Year – *People Stuff*

'As someone who has experienced the collaborative culture of the Sherpa when it comes the climbing in the Himalaya, it's refreshing to see a book which translates these lessons into everyday life advice for those of us in the Western world. There are so many lessons from these amazing humans and Jade captures that perfectly. A highly recommended read for anyone aiming to be the best version of themselves and to be a contributor within their own teams.'

Alyssa Azar – Double Everest summiteer (2016 and 2018). Youngest woman to summit Mt Everest from both the North and South Routes

'*What my Sherpa Taught me About Teams* provides pragmatic insights to leadership and engagement. Through lived experiences and observations, including a once-in-a-lifetime trip to Everest Base Camp, this practical and entertaining book reveals important lessons, many of which have both professional and personal application. I for one will try to remember to "live in the journey"!'

Karin Eden – Group Human Resources Manager

'Engaging storytelling combined with powerful insights. This is the perfect book for anyone involved in developing high-performing teams or who wants to create a career they love.'

Jen Brown – High Performance Coach and host of the *Sparta Chicks* podcast

'The wisdom of a Sherpa goes a long way to combatting burnout. Jade Lee sums this up really well in her new book.'

Mark Butler – Mental Health Strategist and international Amazon bestselling author of *What the Hell Do We Do Now?*

'What a wonderful book! An entertaining yet informative take on employee engagement with a clear and profound analogy to describe the various levels of engagement. As an HR professional who has worked in many different organisations, aiming to increase engagement is always a priority and I will absolutely be referring to this book going forward.'

Karen Zalewski – People and Culture Business Partner

'This book combines vital elements of being a good human with the importance of collaboration to achieve any team goal. Jade encapsulated the essence of the Sherpa and translates their strengths to our modern world. The lessons in this book will help any team member get greater engagement from their work.'

Glenn Azar – Founder of the 'Building Better Humans Project', podcast host, inspirational speaker and adventure leader

'Thanks for bringing your valuable lessons about leadership together with the wisdom of north-east Nepal. I love the use of the mantras! If there's a mountain in an organisation that needs to be climbed, this is undoubtedly the how-to guide.'

Shane Williams – Technology Leadership Expert and host of *The Platform Diaries* podcast

'A refreshing and thoughtful read on the corporate environment full of first-world problems, viewed through a Sherpa's fresh eyes, clean heart and patient disposition. Incorporating concepts from this book would certainly improve an organisation's value proposition to their employees.'

Karen Graham – Senior Talent Acquisition Advisor

'*What my Sherpa Taught Me about Teams* was a lot of fun! With more people working from home than ever before, it's critical to know how to establish and sustain engaged, connected teams. So many leadership books are pure theory, but I found this to be both thought-provoking and practical. I'm excited to put some of the ideas and suggestions provided into practice; this is a book I would recommend to leaders who want to increase team engagement and create genuine connections.'

Kate Silverback – Head of People and Culture

For my Sherpa, thank you Gobinda for carrying my
pack up and down the mountain of life and supporting
me through good times and more challenging times.

In memory of my Mum, I hope this book makes you
proud – an author in the family!

To all my friends and family, immense gratitude for
welcoming my Sherpa into our lives.

Front cover photo from left to right

Lauren Heatley McNeil, Matt McNeil (The Texans), Sijan Dahal (Turbo – he was one quick Sherpa), Drea Sandimaier (The Canadian), Gobinda Dhakal, Jade Lee. Photo credit: Tej Puri.

Inside cover photo

Jade Lee and Gobinda Dhakal. Photo credit: a random trekker on the Annapurna Circuit.

CONTENTS

PREFACE

Have you ever found yourself uninterested in your work?

Not clear if your job was aligned to your real purpose?

Looked back and wondered what happened to your promising career?

Found it hard to get out of bed?

Or achieved all of your goals and wondered why you were not fulfilled?

In December 2014, these were some of the problems I found myself facing.

I had been climbing the corporate ladder for years, while amassing an enviable investment property portfolio and working for some of Australia's biggest corporates – hell, one of them was actually known as the 'Big Australian'. But despite all the appearances of success, I was – as I feel many people in Western cultures are in their late 30s and early 40s – completely disillusioned by what I was doing and what value I was adding to my company and its employees. I was working as a Talent Manager, sourcing and promoting people into roles that the business needed to be filled to realise its goals. I was assisting people to get their dream jobs, but I was increasingly concerned about whether I was really making a positive difference in these people's lives or simply signing them up for an experience that was not going to offer any more fulfillment than their previous position. When you are an individual who believes in living by your values, it becomes difficult to encourage people to come to an organisation where you no longer believe in the culture, the vision, the leadership or the contribution individuals can make.

I vividly remember driving back to my house in Brisbane from my parents' place after a lovely weekend away, dogs in the back of my Toyota Echo, when an epiphany hit me. I was a regular at my local bowls club, and I would stop by and have a chat to the old-timers on my way home from work and had also made friends with the 21-year-old bar tender. He had been discussing his plans to backpack through Thailand, and I was feeling nostalgic about the years I had spent backpacking through Europe in the early 2000s before I even owned a mobile, back when backpacking really was an unknown adventure. I'd had to set up a Hotmail account (that I still use to this day) before I left Australia because email was such a new thing. While driving and listening to an audiobook that clearly was not keeping my attention, I was thinking, *I wish I could just pack up and take off and travel like I could when I was 21.* Then it hit me like a freight train ... *what exactly is stopping you, Jade?* I was already going on a trip to Vietnam and Cambodia in the near future, so I decided to take additional leave from my job and extend the holiday to six months. Still to this day I have no idea why I looked at a map of Asia and decided that Nepal was not that far from Cambodia (as only an Australian could) – I decided to include a side trip to the Himalayan nation and trek to Everest Base Camp.

A GOAL AND A BACKPACK

I arrived with a goal, a backpack and not much else. It was a lofty goal; I had not trained for the expedition, I had not booked a tour, I had one night's accommodation arranged (with an airport transfer included for the bargain price of A$13), and I was ill-prepared for the chaos that is Kathmandu airport. I managed to track down my transfer driver Ramesh outside the airport (an interesting idiosyncrasy of Kathmandu airport is that unless you are travelling you are not allowed inside). He was proudly holding a piece of corrugated cardboard displaying my name from across the road, and he grinned from ear to ear when he realised he had found his client.

As is to be expected when travelling in a developing country, Ramesh had a friend who owned a restaurant, one who owned a trekking store and, most importantly, a friend who was the best travel agent in Thamel (the tourist area of Kathmandu) – an amazing feat as there were over a thousand other travel agents among the hectic bustle who were also the best travel agent in Thamel! Unsurprisingly, Ramesh lost no time in introducing his newest client to all of them in the hope of getting a kickback if I made a booking. Before I knew it, I was flying to Lukla, the most dangerous airport in the world, with a seemingly ill-equipped yet very good-looking Sherpa and an assurance that after the air crash investigations the baggage handlers no longer overloaded the small planes!

After surviving the landing we stopped for some breakfast. We met up with a couple from Texas whom my Sherpa had encountered on a previous trek; they would follow us for the journey. My Sherpa repacked his backpack into mine (so he would only have to carry one bag, he said – although it seemed overly familiar to me) and I was introduced to the slow pace of the trekking life. Breakfast alone took two hours.

Although I had spent six weeks lolling on beaches and in buses, once we finally set off I was keen to show my fitness. I took off from Lukla at a pace my guide was surprised by given my short stature. We arrived in Phakding – where we were to spend our first night – very ahead of schedule and we had some time to fill. It was becoming abundantly clear that this Sherpa, whose name continued to escape me, was interested in more than just taking me on a trek through the Himalayas, and after convincing me to partake in some rice wine after our delicious evening meal we began a holiday romance that would impress any Mills & Boon novelist.

Along with the Texans, an Australian couple, an Australian man, a Canadian young lady and their two Sherpas would become our trekking team. Along the trekking trail – by some form of osmosis it seems – you often find a group of travellers that just works, or perhaps I was just lucky. Our crew, who thought it was odd that my Sherpa and I were happy to bunk in the same room but were too polite to mention it, developed a close connection and had many laughs, and all reached Everest Base Camp unscathed.

We did not however arrive back to the hustle of Kathmandu as the same people. The trip taught us the value of patience (you can't hurry a Sherpa), kindness (looking out for everyone on the trekking trail) and living in the moment. We marvelled at how those who had so little in the foothills of Sagarmatha (the Nepali word for Mt Everest) were happier than almost any of the people from our rich homelands. I learnt how to enjoy the unexpected, let go of preconceived ideas and appreciate the splendour in each breath I took along that trek (although some were more difficult than others). I also got the best gift of all; that good-looking Sherpa is now my husband. His name is Gobinda, and his presence in my life reminds me every day to be patient and kind and to let go of the hurried lifestyle that is so easy to slip into in Australia.

Bringing Gobinda to Australia to start a new life has provided a unique perspective on the intricacies, challenges and indeed self-centred behaviour so common in Western workplaces. I have combined this perspective with 20 years of human performance experience to develop this book, which details the importance of connecting teams in corporate workplaces, how to improve collaboration, reduce employee turnover and ultimately have more engaged and productive employees.

PART I

EMPLOYEE ENGAGEMENT

ONE

WHY EMPLOYEE ENGAGEMENT MATTERS

'It is not the mountain we conquer but ourselves.'
Sir Edmund Hillary

STRIVING FOR THE SAGARMATHA SPIRIT

My reason for writing this book is twofold. Firstly, it has been proven time and again that engaged employees contribute more effectively to companies, and a method for creating more cohesive and productive teams will be of interest to most leaders and organisations. This book will provide practical guidelines and lessons to help leaders engage those in their teams to contribute more fully. However, for me, the biggest driver behind writing this is to support leaders and individuals to become more engaged in their work. We are at work for at least eight hours a day, and with some companies' expectations or an individual's addiction to work, this often extends to ridiculous hours where we are checking email at all waking hours and then dreaming about work at night. We should at least be having happy dreams about how fulfilled we are from the effort we are contributing.

A staggering number of people are not engaged in their work. According to the Gallup State of the Global Workplace report 2021, only 20% of employees worldwide are engaged in their work. The other 80% of us are getting up each day and just going through the motions to get paid. In addition, far too many of us determine our self-worth from our work; the question 'who are you?' is often met with an occupation. If we are not engaged with our work, what does this do to our confidence, sense of wellbeing and connection with ourselves? This is contributing to the growing rates of depression and mental health concerns in our Western world.

How is it that professionals driving their brand-new SUVs off to work in air-conditioned high-rise palaces and going home to McMansions are less fulfilled in their lives than people who are paid $25 a day to carry 30kg packs on their backs trekking up the Himalayas wearing only flip flops?

What are we doing wrong? Does money, status and keeping up with the Joneses not make us happy? It seems so. This will be investigated in this book, along with the role of connection, contribution and support in guiding levels of engagement:

▲ How do we get teams to work better together?
▲ How do we encourage a group of people to collaborate to achieve a goal?
▲ How do we get people more engaged in the work they are doing, the organisation and the vision?

- How did we get so off the track that we are more interested in workplace gossip than whether someone is having problems we should be asking about?
- When did we start straying away from creating a life that aligns with our values?
- And most importantly, how can we get back there?

The lessons from a Sherpa will guide you back to the path of greater engagement at work.

EMPLOYEE ENGAGEMENT IS A SPECTRUM

Working at altitude is tough; when climbing at heights of 3000m above sea level and higher it's important that humans acclimatise. This necessitates a frustratingly slow ascent, during which the Sherpa passes through the same camp many times in preparation to summit Mt Everest.

We know that only 20% of people are engaged at work, so the question is, what are all the other people doing? Engagement is a spectrum; it is not a simple binary equation where you are either engaged or not engaged. The Sagarmatha Spirit Engagement Ladder overleaf demonstrates what individuals are feeling and the behaviours they are exhibiting at each altitude of the employee engagement spectrum.

THE SAGARMATHA SPIRIT ENGAGEMENT LADDER

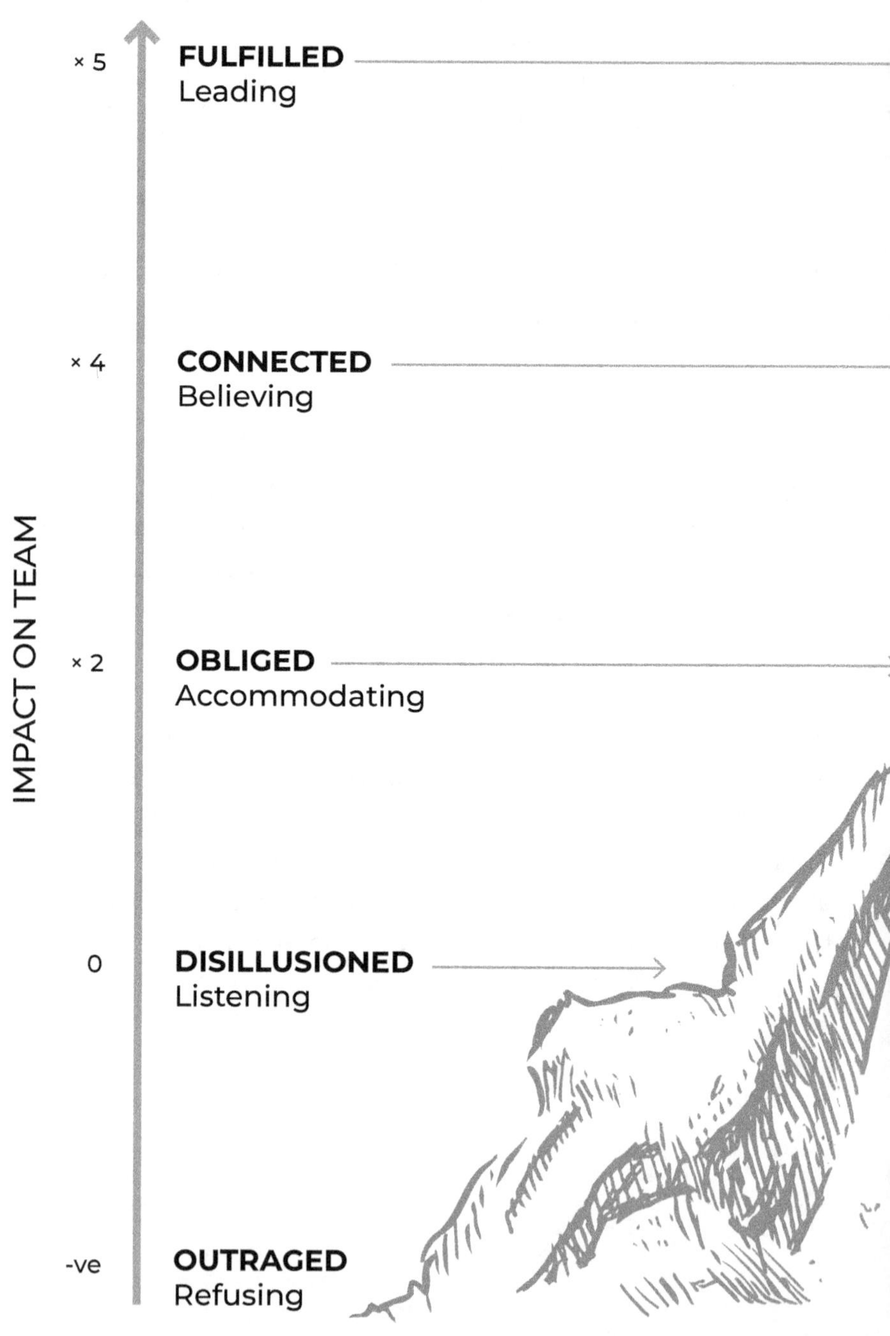

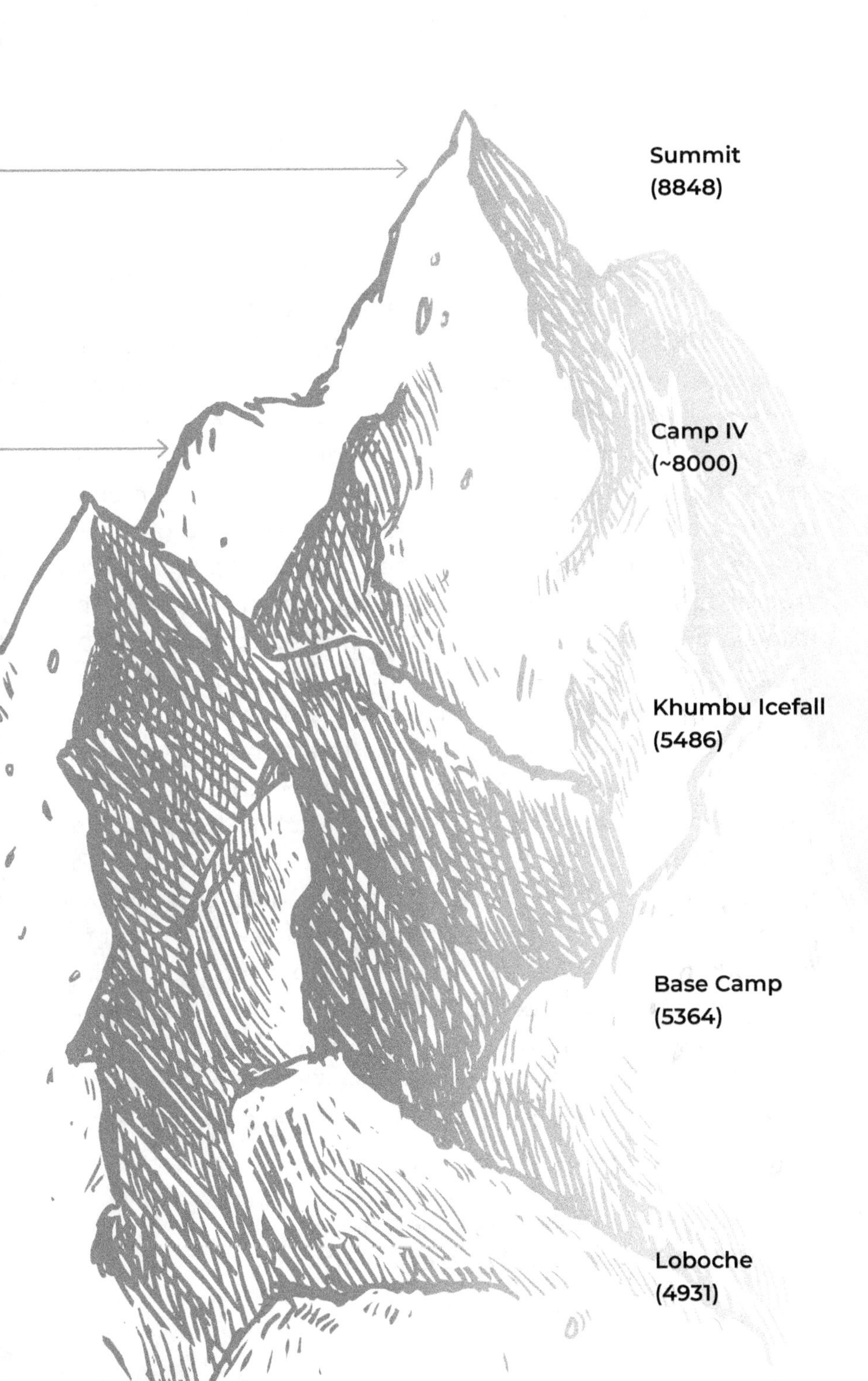

Summit
(8848)
Camp IV
(~8000)
Khumbu Icefall
(5486)
Base Camp
(5364)
Loboche
(4931)

Let's break it down so you can really feel into the emotions and impact that is being experienced at each altitude.

Outraged

In 2014 there was a revolution at Everest Base Camp – it happened soon after an avalanche killed 16 Sherpas. The surviving Sherpas were being encouraged to continue the climbing season by the expedition leaders. The Sherpas felt little thought was being given to their welfare or traditions, and a few of the more rebellious among them initiated the discontent that spread through the camp. Although the Sherpas needed the money, they made a stand against the government (which profits considerably from their work) about their conditions and concerns around safety. It transpired that an agreement could not be reached between the Sherpas, the expedition companies and the government, and as such, the season was cancelled. Because of a few revolutionaries everyone lost the season's earnings and the trekkers missed out on a chance to attempt the summit. Without the Sherpas, there is no possibility of climbing.

In Western workplaces when the team culture is at this point the environment is like 'The Hunger Games' – it's everyone for themselves. There is no support from colleagues, and they will push you off the mountain for a promotion or take the credit for the work of others. This environment is more common during times of restructure or economic downturn. And when people feel unheard and like they are a commodity, they feel scared for their job and psychologically unsafe. The team cannot pull together to have a meeting without argument and backstabbing, let alone climb a mountain.

Mantra in this environment:
WATCH YOUR BACK

Disillusioned

The Sherpas are resisting getting up and getting back to trekking. They do not see the point. Why are they doing this job? There must be a better way to feed their families. Why are they risking their lives for these foreigners? *Is this the work that I am supposed to be doing? Surely there is something better, but I am not sure what that is. What is my end game? I used to love this work, but I am not sure that I do now.*

This is a confusing environment; people are ready to give up but are also looking for a reason to stay. They do not feel any connection to their role or the people they are working with. Everything seems to be too hard, and they do not have the energy to care. They are not sure where to find the answers to their concerns or how to find the way to the sense of purpose they are striving for. The environment is one where the employees may have had a history of feedback falling on deaf ears; they are tired, worn out and are really wanting to hear something that will stop them from spiralling further into discontent. They don't think anything will change but still have an ear to the ground because they want things to improve, although they may not have faith that it will and will likely show suspicion of anyone trying to improve things. They are also likely questioning their own ability but will not admit it for fear of negative consequences.

Mantra in this environment:
SHOW ME THE WAY

Obliged

Crossing the Khumbu Icefall is the most dangerous part of the Everest trek. The Sherpas have to do it many times while transferring supplies. First, they prepare the icefall for safe travel with ladder bridges. They know this work is necessary and they are doing it as well as they can in the pursuit of safety. When they are preparing for a mountaineering party to traverse a moving glacier there is a lot that is out of their control. But they need the money and need to return to their families, so they do what they have to.

These are some common feelings in Western workplaces when people are in this type of environment:

- I need this damn job so I will do what is required of me and nothing more.
- I am wearing the golden handcuffs that were put on when I started earning my high salary.
- If someone came to me and offered me another role, I would take it, but I don't even have enough energy to start looking.
- I don't have to do much work to look good and I only need to cruise along in second gear.
- It is a culture of mediocrity – no one is striving to succeed.

Team members are unlikely to leave such situations of their own accord and have become good at simply surviving. Performance management will not work on them because they will do what is required and no more. The team would love to be lifted up and feel like they are contributing but they will not get there on their own.

Mantra in this environment:
GO WITH THE FLOW

Connected

We have prepared the Khumbu Icefall, and set up Camp I and Camp II. We have been at this for over a month now, ascending and descending the mountain and through the icefall, and we have made it to Camp IV! We are starting to coordinate well as a team, and we are getting a sense of achievement from the work we have already done. Some of us are better at building than climbing so we are getting the best people in the right jobs. From here we can see the top of beautiful Sagarmatha, Goddess of the Sky, and we are starting to get excited about reaching the summit, but the hardest most exhausting part is still ahead.

We have spent a lot of time with the team, and we are laughing and singing together over the campfires when we are at Base Camp. We feel like we know each other better from exchanging stories and looking at pictures. We have mastered the art of communication without speaking when this is required on the mountain.

We know we can achieve more together than individually. I am committed to strengthening the team and contributing my efforts to complement those of the team. I have identified where I can support others and they are willing to accept my help. Not only do I know the strengths and weaknesses of the collective, I know everyone as an individual and what makes them tick, and who the best person is to go to if there is an issue.

Mantra in this environment:
LET'S DO THIS

Fulfilled

Reaching the summit of Mt Everest is a feat only a few people in the world will ever achieve. The odds were stacked against us; there is only a short summit window, and to make it is a monumental effort combined with a bit of luck. Standing at the top, the feeling is pure elation. We all knew what we had to do and why, and we executed. Now we just have to keep this level of support for each other as we descend, but that can be the toughest part. We will leave most of the celebration until everyone is safely off the mountain.

These are some common feelings in Western workplaces when people are in this type of environment:

- We have a team with the intrinsic belief that no one will get there unless everyone gets there.
- We believe in the collective and will do anything to keep this team together, even take a pay cut.
- These people are considered family – I will never be the same for having contributed to this team.
- We can achieve anything we set our minds to because we support each other, we are connected and each of us is behaving as a leader.

Mantra in this environment:
WE ARE ONE

KEEP PUTTING ONE FOOT IN FRONT OF THE OTHER

An employee's emotional attachment to the vision, leader, organisation and work they are doing is what drives their level of engagement. Knowing that engagement is a spectrum and employees can move up and down depending on any number of variables allows us to understand how our team members may be feeling and help them when they need it. Leaders in a team can make a difference to engagement by articulating what needs to be done to reach goals in a sustainable way.

Using the Sherpa analogy again, team members climb up and down through the levels of altitude many times before they summit the mountain. You must spend time at higher altitudes to get your body and particularly your brain used to functioning with less oxygen, and then return to a lower altitude to recover. Each time you ascend you will go a little higher to train the body again and then return to a lower level. You need to travel through the Khumbu Icefall many times to get up to Camp I, and spend time at Camp I and II while becoming acclimatised to the altitude.

Sherpas are not as attached to the altitude as they are to the direction. If they keep putting one foot in front of the other, even if it is descending, they will eventually (God willing) reach the summit. They also have an acceptance that if they do not reach it, that is okay. They hold on tight with an open palm, all the while knowing that if the team is not connected and leading each other and themselves they will not make it.

At work, we will never have a team that is always fulfilled. At any point team members can be on different altitudes of the engagement spectrum. Something annoying may happen to drive one member down, and another member may recognise that and support them to come back up. We are humans with lives outside work which will impact us at work. Clients will change their minds, deadlines will shift and shit will happen, but when we have a strong, cohesive and engaged team we can get through the day to day with a smile on our face and a spring in our step.

Engaged employees are safe and productive employees. Brewing company Molson Coors underwent a program where they focused on improving employee engagement and found that employees who are highly engaged are five times less likely to have a lost time injury. By focusing on strengthening employee engagement they saved the company $1,721,720 from lost work time in one year. Safety and cost savings are an added incentive to investing in employee engagement, and it is everyone's role to contribute to this.

Tenzing Norgay was the Sherpa on Edmund Hillary's successful summit bid in 1953 and is to this day the most famous Sherpa. Such was the teamwork of these two mountaineers that they refused to say who summitted first as they knew that neither of them could make it without the other. That's the thing about leading like a Sherpa: it is important that we all get there … not who gets there first.

SOME STATISTICS ON ENGAGEMENT

'The beatings will continue until morale improves.'

Anonymous

There are many good reasons to be making an effort to improve engagement in your teams, whether you are the team leader, the CEO or the receptionist. Humans crave fulfilment, which comes from knowing you are making a valuable contribution to something each day. When you have a group of highly engaged employees, they will feel connected to each other, believe in the company and be dedicated to the cause.

Across modern workplaces employees are subjected to employee engagement surveys, often at far too regular intervals. Human Resources, People & Culture, People Group, People & Experience departments – or whatever name is trending at the moment – are seemingly only focused on how to increase the 'engagement score', as if subjecting the workforce to more surveys will beat them into submission. Why is that? Why is everyone so intent on increasing workplace engagement scores? Is it just to tick a box as so many initiatives seem to be, or is there a method to the madness?

Employee engagement is the unsung hero of business success. The statistics on engagement – or should I say, lack of engagement – in our organisations are eye opening at best and horrifying at worst. In case I need to convince you that we should be looking at levels of engagement more closely and putting steps in place to improve them, I will highlight a few key statistics that would push anyone into action.

As mentioned previously, according to the Gallup State of the Global Workplace report 2021, only 20% of employees globally are engaged at work, meaning they are highly involved in and enthusiastic about their work and workplace. They are psychological 'owners', drive performance and innovation, and move the organisation forward. The definition of 'not engaged' employees is that they are psychologically unattached to their work and company. Because their engagement needs are not being fully met, they're putting time but not energy or passion into their work. This is a 'go with the flow and take home the dough' approach to work – a term I first heard at a mine site. I was mortified at the saying, but I now realise that unless companies actively invest in creating an engaged workforce, this is all they can expect. 'Actively disengaged' employees aren't just unhappy at work, they are resentful that their needs aren't being met and are acting out their unhappiness. Every day, these workers potentially undermine what their engaged co-workers accomplish. They are down at the disillusioned and possibly outraged altitudes of the engagement mountain.

Interestingly, despite being unengaged at work, Australians and New Zealanders have a very high overall life satisfaction rate of 57%, compared to 32% globally. Happy with life, not happy with work; employees are spending a great deal of their day being less happy than they know is possible. This is not sustainable.

A significant part of the population is on the road to burn-out: 45% of employees report feeling stressed a lot of the day. However, highly engaged teams experience 41% less absentee-ism and 24% less employee turnover. Presenteeism is another cost to businesses. This is when employees physically show up to work, but due to exhaustion, burnout, lack of engagement or poor mental health, their productivity levels are down. This is estimated to cost the Australian economy alone $24 billion each year. This is getting worse, and will continue to do so with the growth in remote working where some employees are just 'moving the mouse' to fool the computer (and their manager in another location) that they are working. Globally, employee engagement decreased by two points, from 22% in 2019 to 20% in 2020, following a steady rise over the last decade. This is likely caused by the pandemic prompting employees to eval-uate their purpose and the fact that they were disconnected from their teams. As engaged business units achieve a 10% increase in customer ratings and a 20% increase in sales, are 21% more profitable and see a 17% increase in productivity, this decrease in employee engagement has a lot of organisations searching for ways to connect their employees with the organ-isation and team.

BEING PRESENT

When you are fully present in any situation, you are engaged. Creating an environment for people to be less distracted will improve engagement in any workplace, and – interestingly – it also increases productivity because people are focused on one task and doing it well.

Humans crave social connection, and unfortunately the connection that we are fooled into believing we derive from social media is not only insufficient, it is often detrimental to achieving real connection. The dopamine hit we receive when someone likes one of our posts leaves us craving the next hit.

In an interview, Sean Parker, the founding president of Facebook, explained that the social media giant's main objective was to consume as much of your conscious attention as possible. This mindset led to the creation of features such as the 'like' button that would give users 'a little dopamine hit' to encourage them to upload more content. He admitted that:

> It's a social-validation feedback loop … exactly the kind of thing that a hacker like myself would come up with, because you're exploiting a vulnerability in human psychology.
>
> It literally changes your relationship with society, with each other. It probably interferes with productivity in weird ways. God only knows what it's doing to our children's brains.*

If consuming our conscious time is the aim of the social media giants, they have certainly achieved it. Look around

---

* https://www.theguardian.com/technology/2017/nov/09/facebook-sean-parker-vulnerability-brain-psychology

at any restaurant in the cities across the globe and you will see people who have sat down to dinner consumed by their phones, not even looking at another person longer than the time it takes to order the meal. When we add in the time that our work zaps from us through our phone and checking the weather, news, messages and sports scores, we are spending a lot of time with a device when we could be cultivating more meaningful relationships.

Along the trekking trail I was obsessed with asking how long … how long to the next village, how long till we stop for lunch, how long till we stop for the night and I can charge my phone, get some Wi-Fi and post about this amazing adventure I'm having? I get how we can believe that posting about something is more important than living it – but my Sherpa certainly didn't. His response to my 'are we there yet?' questions was always noncommittal. ' … 30, 40 minutes … ,' he would say. I was thinking, 'Which is it? 30 or 40? Surely you can tell me at least that? Would you turn up to a meeting 10 minutes late? Would you expect the bus to be there 10 minutes after it's due? How can you be on time for a plane, buddy?' Then it dawned on me: time really didn't matter to these beautiful people. There would always be another bus no matter where you were meant to get to. At the end of the trekking day, there would be a hot ginger tea and curry waiting for you on the stove, anticipating your arrival. You would sit down and chat to your hosts for an hour before being shown to your room or given some sustenance. A few minutes here or there made no difference.

It wasn't that my Sherpa could not give me a specific answer; it was that he *really didn't care*. He was too busy soaking up the experience of trekking through the Himalayas and staring at his beloved mountains and being genuinely interested in the conversations with his clients, learning more about the world outside of Nepal. Although by his own admission he did not love everything about trekking life, he was still truly engaged in the experience. He felt grateful for the life he was living as he was more blessed than many in Nepal, and he found aspects of the work engaging and focused on them. He was aware that his job was to get his clients safely to their destination and back, and have them love the experience so much that they recommended his services to others.

When my Gobinda started working in Australia, to say it was a culture shock would be an understatement. I feel it is important to give him full credit here; he took it all in his stride and one step at a time, but it is bloody hard learning a new country's work customs. There were the obvious differences to his previous work. He had to dress more professionally, be on time and had a boss who was with him every day. However, the real struggle that I underestimated was having to navigate the workplace politics.

My Sherpa would come home and ask me if people might be upset that he was working too hard … 'I think they might be jealous,' he would say. I contemplated … if you are a casual cleaner who is going with the flow and a new person comes in trying their best, impressing the boss and getting more hours, it is likely you would be upset, but I was in a quandary. I did not want him to be paranoid, and part of me thought that the person who is trying their hardest should be rewarded.

Another time he was told by a supervisor that he was not getting as many rosters as another person because the other person was from the same country as the supervisor. Gobinda did not know that this is illegal in Australia (leading to a lesson on the ole Anti-Discrimination Act), and perhaps with my knowledge of workplace legislation it made it harder for me to witness this transition to the Australian workforce.

He worked for a labour hire company who every week managed to get his pay wrong, always less than he was entitled to. He would never have known if I was not referencing the award in the background and correcting the mistakes. Unfortunately, many people who are starting a life in a new country do not know what they are entitled to.

These types of experiences of an innocent man who was trying to make a success in a new country firstly upset me but then got me thinking. These workplace politics and instances of unfairness is something that we all encounter, but does it need to be so complicated? Should it not be enough to come to work, do your job with the best interests of your team and the company at heart, and then walk away knowing you had done a fair day's work for a fair day's pay? How much time would we save by staying out of workplace drama, focusing on our tasks and working more collaboratively? This is the way of the Sherpa, and is one way to have greater happiness at work. Watching my Sherpa navigate our employment landscape was a major motivator to write this book. I believe it is possible to change the approach, reduce drama, and increase the engagement in our work teams.

TWO

WHAT IS EMPLOYEE ENGAGEMENT?

'If you look after your staff, they will look after your customers, it's that simple.'

Richard Branson

My great uncle used to say 'look after the pennies and the pounds will take care of themselves'. This can be translated to 'look after your employees and the business will take care of itself'. When employees are:

- interested in the work that they are doing
- connected to those they are working with
- committed to achieving the vision ...

... they will be enthusiastic about coming to work. They will have direction and meaning in their day and will gain happiness from their connection to others; in short, they are engaged. With this level of engagement, they consider the organisation as their own business. They are invested in its success and are passionate about the contribution they are making.

The power of engaged employees is immeasurable – they will not want to leave, and will encourage other high performers to join them. They will work together to go further; they will give the discretionary effort that will ultimately set your organisation apart from your competitors. Find out what makes your people tick and then give them what they need to thrive.

THE EMPLOYEE ENGAGEMENT MODEL

The following model depicts the ingredients that are required for engagement. These can be applied equally for individuals and teams.

The Employee Engagement Model

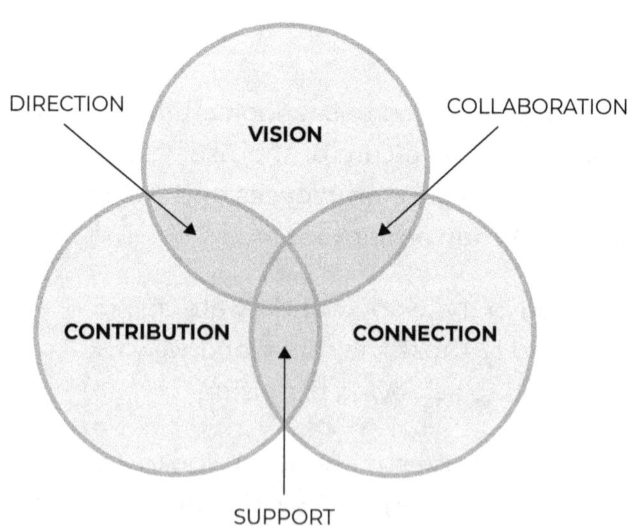

For a team to be engaged, which in turn makes them contribute to the organisation more productively, they need these six aspects (in no particular order).

Vision

They know where they are going, why they are going there and how it will feel when they get there.

Connection

Being connected to the vision, culture and team members. A feeling of belonging to something bigger than themselves.

Contribution

A sense of purpose and knowing how the individual contributes to the collective; a clear understanding of who is responsible for each task; and a feeling of being productive.

Collaboration

They have a camaraderie with those they are travelling with, a knowledge of their strengths and weaknesses, and the ability to freely communicate with them.

Support

A belief that everyone in the team has their back. Being free to make a mistake or have a bad day. Knowing other people will help them when they need it, without judgement.

Direction

Being guided to the destination knowing that there is a conviction of purpose through the tough times.

When these six ingredients of employee engagement are covered, the business is benefiting. It is simple: engaged employees will lift your business to new heights. But, how do you engage them? This is a question we have contemplated for centuries, and as such it's prudent to look back on ancient teachings to shine light on part of the answer.

An essential aspect is to structure the business so that the leaders have time to be fully present with their team. Employees feel valued when their leader is genuinely invested in their success. This also leads to having adequately resourced teams, where people can take the time to develop the connections that will keep them engaged.

FOSTERING ENGAGEMENT ACROSS THE EMPLOYEE LIFECYCLE

If we think of an employee's tenure in a business like a cycle of life, it follows that at the start of life is when the most support is required – if you nurture and teach an infant, they are well equipped to fit in to the community as they get older. They know what is expected, and have been taught how to behave and trained in what to do in their household. We all know someone who has allowed a young child to behave outside the parameters of societal expectations and ended up with a terrible tween, disengaged teen, and a young adult who is not community minded.

The ability to attract and retain great employees is highly dependent on being able to engage employees at all points of the lifecycle. It's helpful to consider the cyclical nature of an employee's tenure, and that how well each aspect is managed will impact other aspects.

The level of engagement created with a new employee has a direct impact on the attraction of future employees, because your business will develop a reputation for how well people are treated. In addition to asking contacts about the organisation's reputation, prospective employees can look at the reviews of companies in online forums such as Glassdoor and Seek to determine if it is a good place to work.

The way that an employee is exited from the business also impacts how the next person succeeds in the role: when there is a strong handover the next person will be set up for success.

The key stages of the employee lifecycle that you must manage are:

- **Attraction:** The key to attracting the best candidates is having a good reputation in the market. If your employees are engaged, they are more likely to recommend quality candidates to your organisation. A strong employee value proposition is key.
- **Selection:** This includes onboarding and effective management of the probation period. When managers play an active role in onboarding, employees are 2.5 times more likely to strongly agree their onboarding was exceptional.
- **Training:** You must improve performance to the level required for the job and align expectations between the employee and the leader. Only two in 10 employees strongly agree that their performance is managed in a way that motivates them to do outstanding work.
- **Development:** Managers account for an astounding 70% of the variance in their team's engagement. When managers are actively supportive of their team, improving

and providing opportunities and feedback, team members are more engaged.

▲ **Departure:** There must be open communication and the beneficial use of a notice period to set the replacement up for success.

Australian retail giant Woolworths has a saying within their talent acquisition department: 'A candidate for a day – a customer for life'. But I suggest that we would do well to take this one step further: 'Employee for a season, raving fan for life'. We can achieve this when we are open and transparent throughout the employee lifecycle. When expectations and processes are fair and communicated effectively, it is easier to have courageous conversations and be confident in the decisions that need to be made.

According to research by Officevibe 65% of employees said they wanted more feedback. If you would like your team to have better engagement, start by investing early in their development; having regular meaningful conversations will start a productive employee lifecycle that will reap excellent returns. Employee engagement doesn't come from only telling employees what is nice to hear: it comes from being genuinely interested in their development and supporting them to achieve what they desire in their career. Honesty and transparency will get you respectful and engaged employees that sugar-coating never will.

To look through the lens of a Sherpa, they give ongoing feedback because it may ultimately save the person when they are on the side of the mountain. When mountaineering at altitude, the smallest difference in your technique or being aware that something could be unsafe or slow you down on the summit push can influence not only if you summit but if you survive.

ENGAGED EMPLOYEES ARE A POWERFUL BUSINESS STRATEGY

Actively create opportunities for team members to connect with each other; it may just be having communal areas near the kitchen where they can share a coffee, or more structured team lunches or 'bonding' events.

Get clear about the vision and don't keep it a secret; be loud and proud and ensure that everyone knows where they are headed and why. They will work together to help everyone achieve their goal, but when the goal is a secret no one will get there.

Don't forget about your remote employees

All the concepts outlined in this book can be enacted with hybrid or remote teams or employees. The premise of this book is studying the Sherpa teams who are with each other 24/7, so I will not go into detail about the variety of methods I suggest to achieve this. However, it's essential that remote teams are deliberate in implementing the six aspects of the Employee Engagement Model. It has been shown that some time dedicated to face-to-face collaboration and connection is beneficial where possible, however I have worked with a high-performing global team with a dedicated group of professionals who never once saw each other face to face. Thorough engagement can be created with geographically dispersed teams with deliberate actions and creative processes.

WORK–LIFE BALANCE

'The price of anything is the amount of life you exchange for it.'

Henry David Thoreau

I love a quote that gets me thinking. I was sent the one above by a colleague a few years ago and I was conflicted as to what I thought about it. With the experience of a global pandemic under my belt, I have another lens to look through which prompted me to think that encouraging employees to bring more of their home life to their work could offer an advantage to leaders and employers. In 2017, according to Gallup, only 14% of Aussies and Kiwis were engaged at work. This indicates that the greatest hurdle to creating an engaged and flexible work-force is that Australians and New Zealanders are not engaged in their work, and this has been the case since well before the pandemic. We are one of only two regions (the other being Western Europe) that, despite high overall life evaluations, has relatively low workplace engagement scores. Thus, the question must be asked: is the reason so many employees crave work–life balance that their work life is so much less satisfying than their home life?

Research from Robert Walters shows that 67% of professionals in Australia are motivated by a good work–life balance, and the *Australian Financial Review* reported that around 70% of workers believed their productivity working from home was the same or even higher than in the office. Combining all this information, why are we not engaged in our work, and how were we able to move to a remote working pattern so quickly when the pandemic hit without a significant impact on productivity?

The impact of the pandemic was of great interest, as I was already questioning the reasons why we were less happy with our lives than most Sherpas. My theory is that employees are dedicated to making remote working productive so they can spend more time in their lives and less time in their work. The time saved in commuting is a clear win to employees who want to dedicate more time to 'life endeavours'.

These musings led me to question why we are so much more engaged in home than work life. The pandemic has prompted many of us to revaluate our priorities. Earning the six-figure salary and power walking like lemmings into our tall and shiny office buildings to earn enough money keep up with the Joneses may have become less enticing. I am reminded of the happy and contented nature of the villagers in the Himalayas; they have very little in the way of material possessions, but they have smiles that convey an infectious happiness that any human would aspire to.

Perhaps the keys to reinvigorating the connection employees have to their work are:

- revisiting their purpose and the value they are providing
- encouraging sharing more about employees' overall life goals, thoughts and values
- further connecting employees with the company and their leaders, colleagues and purpose by each person bringing their whole self to work.

Interestingly, the results of the same Gallup survey in 2021 showed that employee engagement across Australia and New Zealand had increased to 20%. Is this because they were able to connect more to the aspects of their lives that give them the most pleasure in 2020–21?

'Employees who believe that management is concerned about them as a whole person – not just an employee – are more productive, more satisfied, more fulfilled. Satisfied employees mean satisfied customers, which leads to profitability.'

**Anne M Mulcahy, former chairperson and
CEO of Xerox Corporation**

The reason that Sherpas are so happy may be that their work life *is* their life. They often trek with members of their family and trek through villages where they have friends. On the trekking trail I saw a woman who was tending to the field with a baby strapped to her body. Their work is their life. They do not have to postpone having a family to ensure they have enough money to sustain time off work, like many of us do. It is a life where work is just what you need to do to feed yourself, as opposed to a status symbol to prove to those around you that you are successful.

FREE-RANGE WORKING

At our essence humans like to feel we have choices, believing we are at least somewhat in control of the way we work and live. While in many roles there is not the scope to work remotely, where flexibility is possible, consideration to both the employer and the employee requirements is necessary.

I was talking to someone recently who had resigned from his position after working for the company for over 10 years. His reasoning: he didn't feel he was welcome to work in the office (the company had moved to 'hot desking', and had been vocal about its desire to reduce office space into the future), and he really disliked working from home as it was not his preferred style. Companies who move to remote working without giving due consideration to effects on employee wellness should not underestimate the impact this can have on employee retention. Do not presume that everybody will love this option.

I was involved in the development of activity-based working in one of Australia's largest companies. When we rolled out the initiative, employees were told they had the autonomy to be 'free-range chickens'. Free-range chickens can choose where they roost, lay their eggs and chat with their workmates. Employees were free to work wherever: some days in the office, some days from home, some days from their holiday home, and some people would come into the office at exactly the same time and sit at the same desk every day because that was their choice. A key to the success of the rollout was investing time and resources to completely set up the office and employees for activity-based working. The office was fully redesigned for activity-based working with quiet rooms, couches, breakout areas for casual conversations, meeting rooms with great AV capability, and sit-down and stand-up desks.

There is a difference between offering work from home (WFH) options and offering flexibility. Stanford economist Nicholas Bloom reports findings from an experiment with a Chinese call centre in his TED Talk. The home working experiment led to a 13% performance increase; subsequently they rolled out the option to WFH to the whole firm and allowed employees to select between the home or office. Over half of employees switched to WFH, which led to the WFH gains almost doubling to 22%. When the employees could experiment, learn and then select where they worked, that was when the greatest increases in productivity were realised.

Ultimately, freedom is the goal for us all. The reason we trek off to work is the goal that one day, hopefully in line with our retirement, we are financially free. While waiting for that, the freedom to work where we want, when we want and the way that we are most productive is sought by most employees. This is how we will have the greatest work engagement. However as a strong team there is also a willingness to compromise our own needs for those of the team. Therefore, agreeing to work arrangements as a team is very powerful. Everyone is aware of the reasons the arrangements have been put in place and we can best support each other in making it work. There are some people who are not comfortable working from home all the time, some who need to pick the kids up from school, some who are training for a marathon and would prefer to start at 10.00am on a Wednesday. Flexibility equals choice equals freedom. Allow your team to work more aligned to their home life and priorities, because when you create a team of Sherpas all leading themselves, you will reap the productivity rewards that choice offers.

FROM THE PLACE YOU WOULD RATHER BE

Your attitude and that of those around you goes a long way to determining the behaviour that is acceptable in your workplace and, in turn, the atmosphere created. The Sherpas are a happy bunch. I once asked my Sherpa, 'Why are you so happy?', and he came back with, 'You happy, me happy', and the world's biggest grin. This shows his dedication to customer service, knowing that if I am having a great experience it is to his benefit. I'm unlikely to have a great experience if I'm trekking around with a sad sack.

Also, what is the alternative? If you are not happy, you are sad, miserable, despondent, worried, distracted and disengaged. My Sherpa could be miserable at work but where would that get him? The behaviour of those in the team drives the perception of the team, and in most cases the behaviour is determined by the engagement and level of motivation within the team.

We have all worked with people who should have left their job years ago. And we have seen new employees come into an organisation all eager and positive, just to have that enthusiasm crushed by the reality of the environment in which they are now working. When coaching people, I encourage them to make a choice: is your current reality what you want? If not, change something. We can't all have a job where we are sunbathing with a Corona being served to us in an ice bucket. (I wonder if I can get someone to pay me to do that?) The reality is that you spend a lot of time at work and being frustrated and depressed by the environment is not assisting anyone.

Many years ago, I was managing a team member who always saw the negative in any situation. When we would meet she would always have a complaint (or 10!), some of which had merit and which I addressed to support my team. After a few months, I had the realisation that it did not matter what I did to contribute to improving the situation, the team member would always find fault. I established that she just liked to whine. So, I let her whine but also suggested that implementing a more positive attitude might be helpful. She chose to leave not long after that, which I was not concerned about as I resented the amount of energy she was extracting from both myself and the team.

I saw this quote and it conjured up positive vibes for me:

Work done with a cheerful attitude is like rainfall in the desert.

When we all come to work and are cheerful and friendly, we create an environment where more people want to be. This is a critical step in creating a positive work environment and learning to operate like a Sherpa.

Lessons from a Sherpa

- To be successful we need to know where we are going, who we are going with and how we can contribute to getting there.
- For a Sherpa, trekking is their life; align professional and personal motivations for increased engagement.
- We all need to love the journey, love what we are doing every day, and incorporate our work with our personal values.
- Enjoy the work you do; if you are not enjoying it, change something.
- There is no place freer that the trekking trail, wandering through the mountains breathing the clean air and looking after people – this sense of freedom is a big part of why Sherpas enjoy their role. Find ways to increase sense of freedom in your work.

THREE

LEAD LIKE A SHERPA

'It is better to lead from behind and to put others in front, especially when you celebrate victory when nice things occur. You take the front line when there is danger. Then people will appreciate your leadership.'

Nelson Mandela

Sherpas are generally humble in nature and would not consider themselves to be leaders as such. However, they have the qualities that every leader should aspire to. They provide support to their team to allow them to achieve their goals; they work as hard as everyone in the background and allow the team to take the credit; they have the self-awareness to realise they do not have all the answers; and they have the ability to guide and influence people's decisions.

To lead like a Sherpa you embody the intersections of the Employee Engagement Model (refer back to chapter 2). You provide direction and support while cultivating an environment of collaboration to get the most out of the team and nurture them into being the best they can be.

While Sherpas know they have superior knowledge and abilities on the mountain, they do not make this obvious to the team. To lead like a Sherpa, you are aware that you are not in control of everything; you lead by example and will take an alternate route if the current one is not in the best interests of the team or a team member or if the conditions change; you do not believe that there is only one way to approach a problem; and you listen to the perspectives of others. A Sherpa is a leader who will do any job in the team if required, understands the roles of each team member and evaluates strengths and weaknesses so that the best team is assembled, and is a leader who has your back.

When Tenzing Norgay started climbing with Edmund Hillary, Hillary had a near miss following a fall into a crevasse but was saved from hitting the bottom by Norgay's prompt action in securing the rope using his ice axe. This act led Hillary to consider Norgay the climbing partner of choice for any future summit attempt. When someone risks their life to save yours you have trust.

Fortunately, in the average workplace we do not have to display such intense acts of courage in our teams, but to be respected as a leader, your team need to know that you have their backs and you are willing to put yourself in an uncomfortable position to provide them with support.

It is a Sherpa's role to get the team to the top of the mountain but they neither summit first nor take the glory. The Sherpa knows that it's more important to get everyone safely off the mountain than to get any accolades. A Sherpa is trustworthy, has high integrity and looks out for the good of the team. Great leaders know it is by supporting their team that they will make a difference. The title of manager doesn't make you a leader; a leader is born from unselfish behaviour working towards the greater good and being compassionate towards others.

TAKE YOUR STRONGEST TO THE SUMMIT

In a Sherpa's world the group of people they work with to climb the mountain are a team, not a family. If you are not pulling your weight, are unwell or are just not fit enough you will be dropped from the team. It's not personal. It's about your ability to contribute to the team when they need it most. It is essential that the strongest team is taken to the summit, for the good of the collective.

You cannot choose your family but you can choose your team. In a summit team, you get to know each other, you train together, and when the summit push arrives, the decision is made as to who is selected. For relationships to withstand the team selection there needs to have been a variety of feedback – positive and negative – in the lead up, so everyone knows where they stand. This is the essence of performance management: to be fair and transparent. Contrary to popular belief, it is possible to deliver a negative message in a way that the relationship is sustained, and that is to act with integrity and take the emotion out of the delivery. If constructive feedback has been given effectively over a period, it will not come as a surprise to the individual who is cut from the team – they will take responsibility.

Unfortunately, it's easy when you work with a team every day to start thinking of them as family, however when emotions come into the equation our attention is directed away from focusing on the needs of the wider team. Research gathered for a *Harvard Business Review* article showed that workers preferred to receive constructive (negative) to positive (praise) feedback but it was the delivery that determined how receptive they were. From my experience in workplaces, many leaders fear giving negative feedback even when they know it is accurate. Then of course we have the leaders who are micromanagers and have unrealistic expectations of their staff, and even if something is 90% perfect they will find fault and not show appreciation. One of the best skills you can have as a leader is to be able to give constructive feedback because, although we want to receive it, the fact is that few of us like to give it.

The research showed that 92% of people agreed with the assertion, 'Negative (redirecting) feedback, if delivered appropriately, is effective at improving performance'. When the feedback is delivered in a factual, unemotional way and is linked directly to the needs of the business, this makes the message easier to hear, thus easier to deliver.

Sherpas come from a place of doing the best for the collective. They realise it is their duty to enable everyone to be the best that they can be and providing constructive feedback is part of that. It is not expected that the coach of our favourite sporting team will play someone who is not performing. We expect them to give advice on clear areas of improvement, support their team and maintain relationships, so when the player can offer a meaningful contribution they will slot seamlessly back into the team. The same is true of work leaders – we may just need to develop the skill of having the courageous conversation so that the relationship survives.

CELEBRATE SUCCESSES

A Sherpa leader provides the direction for the team to follow, however they know that there are many routes to get there. They listen to the ideas of the team and suggestions of what might be a better way.

It is the nature of a competitive business and an affluent society to always want more. So you managed to pull a rabbit out of a hat and achieve a seemingly unachievable target? We shall reward you by expecting even more the next time! How demoralising is that! This is a drain on your people, and yet is a very common outcome in business. The target that was set was likely quite challenging, yet this often becomes the new benchmark. That is not fair, motivating, or going to get the best out of your people. Instead, celebrate the success and appreciate the work that was put in. If the team did not meet a difficult deadline, take the time to recognise that it was a stretch target and congratulate the team for getting there even if an extension was required.

The Sherpa knows that each milestone along the trek should be acknowledged as an achievement and celebrated with the team. There is power in recognising the small wins and the incremental rewards along the way to a bigger goal. Take the time to celebrate milestone successes with the team; they are the guideposts to reinforce how amazing it will feel when they hit the final target. In addition, they are a good check-in that everyone is still headed in the same direction.

The ancient Romans placed stone pillars called 'obelisks' along the sides of roadways. Typically, the stones were placed a mile apart. Each 'mile stone' was given a unique number, serving as a mile marker. The purpose of the milestone was to track the distance on the overall journey. Similarly, when working on modern-day projects there are milestones that are placed as checkpoints to ensure that the project is running to schedule and budget. These milestones are pressure points to all of those involved in the job, and quite often the only reward is striving for the next milestone. It is the journey not the destination where we spend most of the time. The Sherpas spend less than five minutes at the top of Everest, an achievement that has taken months or years of preparation. The key is to live in the journey and strive for the achievement.

The living is all in the getting there

If you are always waiting for the destination, you are wishing your life away. It is important to remain present and appreciate where on the trail you are now – being conscious of celebrating the successes along the way is a technique that you can use to do this. It is great to have clear targets; you are exponentially more likely to achieve what is required with targets or goals.

Liz Jazwiec, author of *Eat That Cookie!: Make workplace positivity pay off ... for individuals, teams and organizations*, explains that workplace celebrations foster relationship building, improve morale, enhance retention and encourage employees to achieve results. When you take celebrating team success one step further to celebrating individual successes, you acknowledge the positive impact one member has had on the team achievements. If you position these as success stories you encourage the entire team to reflect on their contributions and this can have a positive impact.

Apart from anything else, celebrating successes is fun; pop the champagne and let the party begin, team! Regularly appreciating the contribution of employees is a motivating practice. It is amazing the efforts that people will invest to meet a deadline but if there is no recognition this energy is quickly lost.

Case study: Project possible

In 2019 a Nepali named Nimsdai 'Nims' Purja – a former Gurkha (the British Army recruits a number of soldiers from Nepal every year and they form the Gurkha regiment) and SAS soldier – made a decision to climb all of the 14 peaks greater than 8000m altitude. He was not a trained Sherpa but had established that he was a good mountaineer and had superior cardiovascular physiology. The quickest anyone had summited the 14 peaks was over seven years yet Nims believed he could do it in seven months. He quit his job, re-mortgaged his house in England and assembled a team of Sherpas to take on the peaks across Nepal, Pakistan and Tibet.

Nims believed in the team. He gave them a detailed plan, and made it clear that they were not completing the mission at the cost of safety. They helped fellow mountaineers in the death zone (above 8000m) – his time in the army had given him the value of 'never leave a man behind'. After summitting all of the Nepali mountains and spending a few nights in Kathmandu for celebrations between summits, they had to take on the technical and highly dangerous challenge of K2 – perhaps the most revered mountain of them all. Many have not survived to tell the tale of their K2 summit attempt.

When they arrived, many who had tried to summit had given up and were packing up to go home. There was too much snow, regular avalanches and one climber described it as 'the mountain was disintegrating below you'. When Nims's team arrived they established that the ropes had not been fixed all the way to the summit – Nims encouraged a few of the defeated mountaineers to give it another go as his team would go ahead in the middle of the night when the snow was rock hard and fix the ropes. This was a bloody dangerous challenge and they were met with quite a bit of resistance from the seasoned mountaineers, who wondered why they thought they could conquer the mountain and the bad weather when they had all failed.

Nims and his team were resolute. They believed in their vision and they believed that they could achieve what they set out to do. The Sherpas and Nims worked tirelessly through the night, summited K2 and fixed the lines, enabling another 40 climbers to summit after them. They went on to summit all 14 peaks (after convincing the Chinese government to keep some of the mountains open after the season had ended) and the story is now a documentary entitled *14 Peaks*. Nims's team was a team of leaders. No one thought that the challenge could be achieved but Nims and his team did. Nims actually called the challenge 'Project Possible' because he was sick of people telling him it was impossible. They achieved the impossible with a leader who provided direction, support and an environment where they could all collaborate. Nims embodies all that it means to lead like a Sherpa.

Mantra:
WE ARE ONE
The culture of fulfilment in a team is the
Holy Grail: that feeling you get when you achieve
something in a team that seemed impossible.

After we returned to Kathmandu from Everest Base Camp, my Sherpa wanted to take me to Pokhara. He told me that it was

Nepal's honeymoon destination. Sure, I thought. Sounds like a great idea for a bit of downtime, and there were many other treks in the Annapurna ranges to explore in the area. He had advised that it was 180km away. Great, should be there by lunchtime, I thought. Silly silly Jade; that is an eight-hour journey in Nepal if you are lucky. The fact that the mountain roads do not enable a small bus to go faster than 40km/h is one constraint (bearing in mind this is a major thoroughfare from Kathmandu to India), but it is also the fact that you are on Nepali time. You will stop every hour for a rest, lunch, breakfast, snack, afternoon tea, coffee – whatever excuse is convenient. You will be stopping often and exiting the bus at a food provider of some description. This is in addition to the regular stops to pick up passengers, which is invariably a 10-minute production of rearranging bags on the roof and moving people around to accommodate a cage of chickens (not even exaggerating). It is like the bus timetable (who am I kidding?) allows for a 30-minute celebration of successfully travelling 40km: good work keeping yourself cooped up in the bus for one hour – you shall now be rewarded with 30 minutes to stretch your legs. With this experience, is it any wonder that my Sherpa wants to stop for coffee 20 minutes after leaving the house on a 350km drive? Even the dogs are trained to not need a rest stop. This drives me crazy, but there certainly is a balance to be struck between living in the moment and driving relentlessly to the destination.

Check in regularly

When we are in pursuit of a vision, the 'how' to achieving the vision may change or need refinement or an entirely different approach. When change happens, it is helpful to co-create a new process with all the team, again in the pursuit of getting buy in. Think through the reason for the change of process and what you would like to achieve from it. From there, collaborate to determine what the new process will be and what the measures of success are. It is not essential that there are key performance indicators (KPIs) established, but if there are going to be repercussions for not achieving something the team needs to know what they are.

When rolling out a new process, including the expectations of what good looks like and tracking progress closely is often overlooked. When team members know where they stand and what is expected of them it offers a level of safety. It is not fair to call out poor performance when the boundaries of what is expected were never established. This is, in effect, setting up the employee to fail. The minimum we can do to enhance our team's psychological safety is provide them with clarity about their role, purpose and parameters that they need to work within.

Sherpas are not wedded to one plan to get to the summit. On the trekking trail, the process or method is continually being evaluated and this may mean that the roles of the team members need to change. The team will have to collaborate to make the new plan work. With the long-range weather forecasts the team is pretty confident of which day they are going to summit, but there are so many variables when climbing at altitude that you can never know what the mountain is going to throw at you. Sherpas have a flexible plan that can be altered at a moment's notice. The issues that can be encountered are endless: someone injures themselves and cannot continue; someone comes down with altitude sickness; an unexpected storm rolls in; a tent blows off the mountain; the oxygen is used more quickly than expected.

In organisations, KPIs are often linked to bonuses or annual remuneration reviews. In my experience, however, these goals are not reviewed regularly. They are often set and forget – until the manager and team member wonder 12 months later why they were not achieved. Dr Edwin Locke and Dr Gary Latham are researchers and authors in goal setting and performance. Locke found that over 90% of the time goals that were specific and challenging, but not overly challenging, led to higher performance when compared to easy goals or goals that were too generic, such as a goal to do your best. Latham studied the effects of goal setting in the workplace. Locke and Latham published in 1990 'A Theory of Goal Setting & Task Performance', stressing the importance of setting goals that were both specific and difficult. Work with your team members to set challenging yet achievable goals, and then support your people to reach them. An essential part of this support is providing the opportunity to regularly review the goals and progress towards them.

Regardless of whether the goals are linked to bonuses, high performers always want to be working towards something. Set the expectations for their day-to-day role but also give them some larger targets to work towards to give them motivation and a sense of achievement. Defining what you expect the team to do is critical for them to achieve it. It may sound overly simplified, but it is a step that is often missed with a new starter or change of role or process.

Alyssa Azar had a goal to become the youngest Australian to summit Everest by May 2014. Due to the avalanche that killed 16 Sherpas in 2014 she was unable to reach her goal, and then she encountered an earthquake in 2015 and the season was again cancelled. She went back in 2016 and summited in May, two months after my Sherpa came to live with me in Australia. I remember being very worried for her, thinking that it was not meant to be, but she knew where she was going and kept checking in that she still wanted to achieve the goal. She also achieved many other things in the two years waiting for her Everest goal to manifest. Leading like a Sherpa you keep slowly chipping away until you get there. She went on to also summit from the Tibet side in 2018, making her the youngest women to summit Mt Everest from both the north and south routes. That is a lot of steps, taken one at a time, one after another.

Lessons from a Sherpa

- Let the team summit first.
- You can lead from the back, supporting people to get where they need to go.
- There are many routes to the same destination – we can change direction.
- The quickest way may not be the best way.
- Know the importance of rest and allow time just to contemplate where you and your team have come from and what is great about the present situation.
- Every small success should be celebrated – it helps us know we are advancing to the summit.

PART II

THE EMPLOYEE ENGAGEMENT MODEL

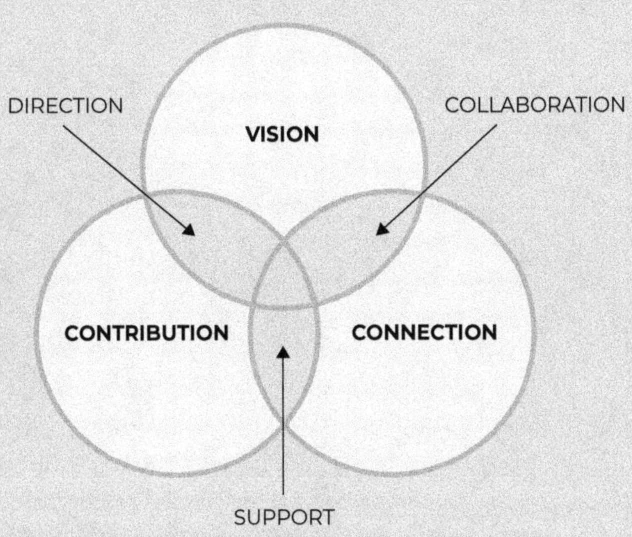

FOUR

VISION

'If you are working on something that you really care about, you don't have to be pushed, the vision pulls you.'
Steve Jobs

The vision of a company – or indeed a team or individual – provides the motivation to achieve each day. It aligns contribution with a direction you are working towards and provides a reason to give your best every day. It has the power to inspire the team towards the same overarching goals and enables a feeling of accomplishment upon reaching them. When communicated effectively, a well-thought-out vision can also promote the company brand and be the basis of an employee value proposition, thereby attracting and retaining top talent.

The more employees feel aligned with the vision and values of an organisation, the higher the chances of them staying the course, assisting to overcome challenges and being happier to contribute.

In a Sherpa's world, the vision is easy to articulate because it is easier to see. The vision is the top of the mountain on the horizon, or the smaller milestones of the next village or camp.

CREATE A VISION THAT YOUR PEOPLE BELIEVE IN

A key component of having an engaged team is to share with them what they are striving for. An effective team needs to know where they are heading and the route they are going to take to get there. The route can be held lightly as there will be obstacles on the path to the vision, which means that the route deviates, but holding the vision close enables those changes to be less derailing.

If you do not know where you are headed it makes it exponentially more difficult to navigate obstacles and stay on course. Gallup's 2013 research showed that less than 41% of employees feel they know what their company stands for and what makes its brand different from its competitors. Disseminate and, if necessary, create a tangible vision that employees can feel and get excited about working towards. Show the team why the vision is important, how it will be realised and what good looks like. Create a vision your team will empathise with.

You would have had to be Nostradamus to have foreseen from February 2020 to where we would be in November 2021, but those with a clear direction in early 2020 of where they were headed and why they wanted to get there still made some headway towards their goals, albeit not following the path they may have envisaged. Their vision was the foundation on which the organisation pivoted to stay on track as much as possible. Those who were floundering pre-pandemic are still floundering, or have deviated from the track altogether and fallen down a crevasse.

Effectively communicating the vision is far too often overlooked. Perhaps there is an assumption that everyone knows the vision as it is on the company website or was communicated in an email six months ago, but something as integral to the motivation of employees as 'knowing their why' (thanks Simon Sinek) should not be left to communication that is easily missed or forgotten. Get some enthusiasm behind your message. Bring the vision to life, make it relevant, use storytelling, gesticulate, smile, get people involved. When talking about the vision, encourage the team to imagine how amazing it will be when they are working at a company that is living its vision. Knowledge of and belief in a tangible vision motivates employees, and makes them more productive and more supportive of others working towards the same vision.

A vision that is slapped on a strategy paper and hidden deep in the intranet offers no value. Make it real. Create a powerful vision your team is in love with, inspired by and obsessed about achieving and they will follow you where the vision leads.

Believing is committed

'Whatever the mind can conceive and believe, it can achieve.'

Napoleon Hill

When faced with a seemingly insurmountable challenge, if your leader believes you can do it, you will believe you can do it and those around you will believe you can do it. There is then a bloody good chance you will get there. That's the way of the Sherpa. I have seen it time and time again: if a team believes in themselves, they will commit to getting a task done, and they will achieve it because they believe it. In the words of an entrepreneur I knew many years ago starting up a business with three colleagues who had mortgaged their homes on the venture, 'Failure is not an option'.

Once you have the right vision and people believe in it and the right people are with you – or more to the point, the people with the right attitude are with you – in the battlefield (let's face it, sometimes when we are chasing down an audacious vision it can feel like a war), you will get it done. You will make the vision reality; you are committed, you are willing to do whatever it takes and support whomever you need to, to meet the goal. There is a reason that the behaviour we see when we are one rung from the top of the Sagarmatha Spirit Engagement Ladder is believing; you are not summiting unless you are believing the team can get there. When you are committed you are willing to put in the work and complete the actions required; you believe in what you are doing and the way you are doing it; and you want to see the aspiration come to fruition. People will follow vision and values when they commit to and believe in them, and the best way to get them committed is to co-create the aspiration with your team.

Getting individual buy in is vital. Your people need to see value in striving for the vision; feel like they belong and that their opinions are valued; and believe that with the support of each other they can get there. The amazing thing about belief is that it is contagious. If you have a leader who is charismatic enough or has enough conviction, this person will spur on the other individuals who then spur on each other.

Believing is contagious and it leads to commitment. Get everyone involved in crafting the vision and guiding principles to get there and you will have their commitment. Once you have that, the sky is the limit.

WHAT'S YOUR TEAM'S POTENTIAL?

I remember in physics class learning about the concept of potential energy. Potential energy in a lot of cases is driven by gravity. We often think when we are at the bottom of the mountain that we have the potential to reach the top, whereas all the metaphors have it backwards. At the top of the mountain is where all the energy lies, in the ability to fall to the bottom driven by gravity.

This applies to individuals, teams and indeed organisations. Every organisation has the potential to have a good culture but (depending on where it is currently at) there is a certain amount of work, discipline and guidance required to realise that potential.

When you look at any image of potential energy you will notice a kinetic force that is acted upon an object before it has the potential energy to continue moving.

The team's potential comes from what they are about to achieve not what they have already achieved. In physics, potential energy is when an object has energy held within it; if it was released the object would move. For example, a coin being held out the window of a tall building has potential energy, or indeed a Sherpa at the top of Everest has potential energy. This energy has been realised through the hard work and effort that it took to get to the top of the mountain.

The same is true in your teams.

We are told from a young age we can do anything we want; we have all the potential in the world, but it is hard work that creates the potential. Unless you first climb to the top of the mountain, you will not have created your own potential energy. In Rory Vaden's bestseller *Take the Stairs*, he theorises that too many people in our society are riding the escalator instead of taking the stairs. He counters that he is yet to meet a successful person who did not achieve their dream lifestyle without paying a price, without sacrifice and without self-discipline. It is the hard work that gives you the potential energy to achieve more. Natural talent will only get you so far; to reach the top of any endeavour requires work.

Have you ever heard of a team being referred to as having potential? What they are really saying is, if they do the work, they will achieve great things. The more work that is invested the more potential energy the team is creating. We all have potential, we can all put in the effort, thus we can all be successful in what we set our minds to (within reason – no matter how much effort I put in, I was never going to be a champion basketball player with my five-foot stature). Which reminds me, my high school Health and Physical Education teacher told me that anyone can be a world champion. You just need to determine the sport best suited early enough, put in the countless hours of training and don't get injured!

The potential for anything is limitless but hard work is required and there needs to be motivation to take action. This is where the vision comes in: the compelling reason to get out of bed every morning, to do the work, to create potential energy, to convert it to kinetic energy and to move towards achievement of the goal.

It is the vision that drives the action that creates the potential energy. There will be a team vision but the individual vision that drives each person's motivation is likely to be quite different. We are all striving to reach the summit – some of us will make it and some won't. Some are going for the sheer thrill of climbing, some to support our families, some for the camaraderie, some for the status of being a Sherpa, some for helping others witness the beautiful scenery of our country.

These are all compelling 'whys' for the individual to bring the vision to life. These whys drive how much potential the individual, and when combined, the team, has to be successful.

Case study: A monumental task

A labour hire company won a very big contract to fill over 300 positions in 20 locations nationally. It was monumental task; they had never recruited for this industry or with as much compliance checking as this piece of work required. The timeframes were hellishly tight, and the Account Manager had very little faith that it could be fulfilled within the terms prescribed; in fact, her experience told her that this was an impossibility. But she loved a challenge and knew that no one else was any more likely to achieve it.

The team she had to deliver the contract was largely new to the industry and was learning on the job. The Account Manager made a point of creating a fun, rewarding and high-performing environment, and imparted a lot of her knowledge to the team. She had said to one particular team member, 'when you have finished this project you will be able to pick up a recruitment job anywhere'. She set up regular team meetings, daily check ins and an online tracking sheet, so everyone knew where they stood and what they had to achieve each day.

The vision was clear: filling all of the roles nationally by the date mandated. The Account Manager was encouraging, positive and supportive. The feeling in the team was one of camaraderie. Everyone was collaborating to make the dead-line, asking for help, learning new things and working on the buzz of filling the positions. As time went on the Account Manager could see they were making ground on the timeline and started to allow herself to think that they might even achieve it.

As some locations were filled everyone rallied to help the other locations; if someone was away from their desk other people would answer their phone to make sure they did not miss any potential candidates; and they even convinced one candidate to relocate to a regional area where they were having difficulty attracting candidates. They met the deadline, and the team went out and had a celebratory dinner. The client was invited. One team member overheard the Account Manager confessing that she had thought it was impossible to complete the project in time. 'What – you never told us that!' the team member accused in an indignant tone, and then started smiling.

Mantra:

LET'S DO THIS

Even if you think it is impossible, give it a go.
Teams who are in the 'connected' rung of the
engagement ladder believe in each other!

ANTICIPATION TRUMPS REACTION

In Stephen Covey's book *The 7 Habits of Highly Effective People*, one of the world's bestselling books ever on productivity, guess what the very first habit is? Be proactive! It's far too easy for people to fall into the trap of reactivity. When working in that space there is no room for strategy.

Using the analogy of firefighters putting out fires:

▲ When there are spot fires everywhere they are in reactive mode.

- When there is a fire alarm, they are anticipating the fire and (hopefully) have time to get to the blaze before it gets out of control.
- When the firefighters are in a completely proactive space, they spend their time back burning to stop a blaze taking hold.

When we can anticipate problems that lie ahead and plan for them, we have a strategy to keep business running as usual. For example, in flexible work teams, when you know the personal situation of your team members you can show consideration for their circumstances and understand what problems might arise. Anticipating problems is not about dreading and worrying about all the things that could go wrong but is instead about giving some forethought to issues that may arise and having a plan for them.

To anticipate problems that may arise you need to have strong knowledge of your team. For example, if we know that Bob finishes at lunchtime on Friday and he has a demanding client group who always leave things until the last minute, have a plan in place where someone can cover for Bob should something arise at 4.45 on Friday afternoon, or better yet give that client group to someone who is happy to push back on their stakeholders and influence them to be more proactive!

Knowing what can go wrong on a mountain is hugely important for staying safe. Some disasters (like an avalanche) are seemingly unexpected, but there are still mitigation strategies that can be put in place. Did you know that avalanches generally happen as the day gets hotter? It makes sense, right? The sun is melting the snow and creating instability. The avalanche that killed 16 Sherpas in 2014 hit at about 11.00am.

Crossing the Khumbu Icefall is bloody dangerous: it is a glacier – or perhaps it's better described as a frozen waterfall – that is 600m tall (the Empire State Building is 381m). To pass it requires climbing vertically at some points, and crossing ladders over crevasses (in crampons) at others. At any time, a block of ice the size of an apartment building could break free above you, or the glacier could move and dislodge the ladders. The Sherpas cross the icefall up to 40 times before they get to the summit as they are preparing the track for others. They are installing ladders, anchoring ropes and carrying oxygen bottles.

The icefall is a glacier that is in constant – albeit very slow – flow. If the glacier moves significantly while someone is crossing, it's very dangerous – most likely fatal. Thus, to reduce the risk of major ice movement, traversing the icefall is typically done very early in the morning. It is more intelligent to avoid a dangerous situation than respond when it arises.

We know we need to cross the icefall to reach the vision, so although we know it's dangerous, we have strategies in place to reduce the peril and it does not stop us from going through many times. The vision of reaching the summit is that vivid.

GET COMFORTABLE BEING UNCOMFORTABLE: IT'S WHERE YOU AND YOUR TEAM WILL GROW

Look around; can you see anyone who has achieved greatness by staying comfortable? Printed in bold letters on the wall at my local gym are the words:

Change Begins Outside Your Comfort Zone

I looked at this quote for years and considered the meaning while doing high-intensity cardio; it was a source of great motivation and contemplation while I was trying to inhale enough oxygen to power my little being to lunge, jump, run and kick my way to an amazing body. I considered that when we are trying to change our bodies there is no way we can build muscle or increase our cardiovascular fitness without being outside of our comfort zone. Such is the truth for anything new we want to achieve in our lives.

To be well known in your field you have to put your ideas out to the world. It may be writing a book, it may be posting on Twitter or LinkedIn, or giving a speech. Oprah Winfrey, Brené Brown and Simon Sinek are all people who have managed to be known for what they do, but they have had to get comfortable being uncomfortable to do so. The same is true for you. If you wish to have a career of note where you make a difference, you will need to get uncomfortable. Sitting in the same seat feeling somewhat stuck will not get you where you want to go. Recognising that you are stuck in your job, or worse yet spiralling downward to complete disengagement, is an important step so that you a can give yourself a shove to make a shift in your career. The first step is to get clarity around your vision and your why for achieving it.

One thing I know for sure is that life is too short to be languishing in a job that you are not engaged with or challenged by. So why are there so many people who are doing just that? I have given this topic a lot of thought and called on my years of managing talent and have determined it is a combination of factors, but the inability to step out of their comfort zone is what stops most people changing.

You also require the ability to sit with the discomfort and evaluate how you feel about it. Yoga taught me how to hold space in discomfort. When you can do that with yoga poses it is a small change to do it with your emotions through meditation. I was teaching a yoga class a couple of months ago and relaying this exact topic. One of my students told me that he was in pain after holding a pose for a couple of minutes. I gently asked if he was in pain (not acceptable) or just discomfort (what we are actually striving for). He replied, 'Let's just call it intense discomfort … ' He was a regular, and he kept coming back for his dose of discomfort as he knew it was helping his flexibility and he appreciated the calming effect it had on his mind.

Change is scary. It is easier to sit at your desk and take home the regular paycheque and pretend you are not being affected by your lack of engagement in your role. However, you are kidding yourself. The only way that situation improves is by you doing something to improve it. You require courage and energy to make a move, and more importantly you will need to do some soul searching to determine exactly what you want from your life – but it certainly will be worth it.

It may not work out … yeah, so what? You gave it a shot. Just because you make a change doesn't mean it will work out perfectly every time. You will, however, have had a learning experience that has given you more data points to determine what you do want.

It's rare that opportunity knocks on the door of a disengaged person sitting in their comfort zone. Get out there and make a change and make the most of this one beautiful life that you have been blessed with; your life is in your hands. It is up to you to create what you desire. Do not wait for your boss, your colleague, your rival in the next cubicle to make it possible for you to achieve your dreams. It does require a bit of self-evaluation to step out of your comfort zone, particularly if you have been in a role or a company for a long time, but you can do it. Find the vision you want for your life. Get clear on it. Know your why. Check in regularly on your vision. Are you on the right track? Do you need to deviate? Is the vision still relevant, or do you need to change some or all of it? Life throws us curveballs, and sometimes what we think we are striving for is actually no longer relevant.

The first step is to get clear on the vision of what you are working towards, know the why, get excited and then get moving.

Lessons from a Sherpa

- Tell your team where they are going, and they will find a way.
- We do not know the obstacles ahead – we need flexibility in the way we get there.
- Your team will do the work needed to get there if they believe they can.
- You believe it is possible because you have seen others achieve it. You know it is tough because you have seen other people fail. You know it is worth it because you have seen the eyes of successful summiteers.
- Keep safe by anticipating problems and trying to avoid risk. Reactivity is a dangerous place to be.

FIVE

CONNECTION

'Connection – The energy that exists between people when they feel seen, heard, and valued; when they can give and receive without judgment; and when they derive sustenance and strength from the relationship.'

Dr Brené Brown

Connection is vital to any team's engagement. In theory, Sherpas should struggle with this more than most teams because they work with a new group of people every few weeks and they are constantly establishing new connections. However, Sherpas have a strong knowledge of teams and what makes them successful; they know that connection is a vital element of this. They know that the greater connection they can create, the better experience their clients will have. Their client could be a 23-year-old female from South Korea on one trek and a 40-year-old Argentinean male the next. Most people who chose mountain guiding as a living are 'people people' – they are infinitely curious about others' stories, how they think and what motivates them. There are many hours of downtime in mountaineering to rest, recuperate and acclimatise to the altitude, which is a lot of games of cards, cups of tea and conversations to get to know each other better.

What Sherpas have on their side is time; they are walking side by side with people for hours each day, they have a lot of time to fill with conversation, and from my experience trekkers are genuinely interested in learning about those they are trekking with. Although it is becoming less so, electricity and Wi-Fi connections are rare on the trekking trail, therefore when groups stop there are few distractions.

The following image outlines the three facets of connection – when each is addressed there is a sense of respect, trust and belonging created in the relationship. When teams feel connected to each other, the organisation and the vision across the social, emotional and intellectual spectrum, they are unlikely to want to leave the organisation, and engagement improves.

When a team is formed or a new team member arrives are the critical times to focus on connection. According to Bonusly's Employee Engagement and Modern Workplace Report 2020, onboarding is an integral time for new employees to connect with a company's culture and people. I have seen time and again when the effort is invested up front the returns for the team are ongoing. We should not underestimate the importance of intentional connection early in the relationship; finding ways to consciously create the connection determines how well the team gels.

Creating strong team connections

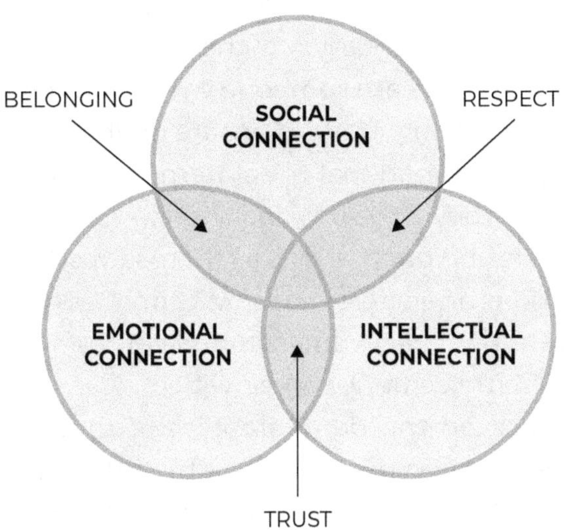

CONNECTING THROUGH TOLERANCE

A culture is made up of behaviours, beliefs, values and motivations of those in the group. In any culture there are certain behaviours that are accepted and encouraged; these behaviours are those that the collective has deemed fair and desirable. The behaviours of one culture may appear to be unusual or even unacceptable to another culture but work for the group that they are a part of. When people from different cultures come together it is important to show tolerance early to develop connection with each other.

While working in the mining industry I was reliably informed that FIFO does not only stand for Fly in–Fly out. 'Really?', I enquired somewhat naively but genuinely interested. A veteran miner with a sly grin on his face stated it also stands for 'Fit in or f*#k off'. I must admit that this response did leave me a little shocked; not the language itself (you do not decide to take a role on a mine site if you can't handle a few expletives!) but more the overall insinuation of the statement. As you may have already guessed, I am someone who values equity in the workplace and I actively work to ensure an inclusive environment. I wrongly assumed that the statement 'fit in or ... there's the door' meant they were only looking to include those with the same beliefs and orientations as themselves, but observations, interactions and altercations over time taught me what the harsh statement really indicated was they were craving connection with those they worked with.

Looking back on the demographics of that mine site it could have easily become a 'boys' club' of the middle-aged, white variety but it was not, because one of the values they held in their culture was tolerance; if you made an effort to have a yarn with others on the site and found something that connected you to each other and you got the job done, that was enough to 'fit in'. They were looking for a level of what they would call mateship but what I call connection, which leads to trust, respect and a sense of belonging. They recognised that diversity and connection were not mutually exclusive. It was as if they enjoyed the challenge of finding connection with people of different backgrounds.

I have also seen this work in a detrimental way in a culture where tolerance was not valued highly. A young professional of Middle Eastern background was brought into a team of Anglo-Saxon middle-aged men and after a short period it was deemed that he was not performing. They wanted to start performance managing him, however I had suspicions as to why he was not performing and suggested that we should give him a chance to improve in another team. I strategically chose a team that was diverse in ages and cultural backgrounds, and was tolerant. The team included a passionate, experienced person who loved to mentor. The young man's performance was not an issue in the new team. When I had a conversation with him about why this was, he told me he now felt heard and was in a team where people valued his contribution and were keen to learn about him as a person.

The first day I was trekking through the Himalayas with my Sherpa headed towards Everest Base Camp, the question of religion came up. He asked me if I was a Christian; despite 12 years of Catholic education I was not comfortable saying yes. I do believe in a greater force I choose to call 'the universe' – I am not a believer in Christ or God as depicted in the bible. I simply replied, 'I believe in being a good person'. To this he replied, 'Yes, me too'.

At high school most of us learnt about different religions, including Hinduism, Judaism, Islam, Buddhism and of course Christianity. At that time, most of us began to understand that all religions have the same basic premise: be good to one another and you will get into heaven, or be good to one another and karma will be kind. There are key beliefs that are by and large consistent through all religions. This is what makes it possible for multiculturalism to be successful, albeit with a certain level of tolerance required at times. Humans at our core generally have the same beliefs and values, meaning we can work well together in most team situations.

The 'beliefs' of one team can be different to that of another team within the same organisation. In one team the belief might be that if they help their colleagues, their colleagues will help them when they need it. Do unto others as you would have them do to you. Whereas in another team the belief might be that people do not support them, so why should they give any support in return? An Old Testament eye-for-an-eye philosophy. This belief will encourage CYA (Cover Your Arse) behaviour. The collective beliefs of a group of people will have an impact on the level of connection fostered in the group – humans prefer to work in a team where the beliefs are around supporting, respecting and valuing each other.

Many workplaces are aspiring to develop a diverse work-force as management sees the benefits diversity brings. Diversity is important according to a study from Massachusetts Institute of Technology because people from diverse ethnic backgrounds, generations, genders, races and religions provide different viewpoints that allow for better problem solving and creativity. This is only beneficial if everyone feels free to express their views and feels that their contribution is valued, and therefore tolerance is so important.

My Sherpa learnt English almost exclusively by talking to tourists on the trekking trail. He loves to know more about people and the countries and politics and religion of the area from which they come. He is knowledgeable and tolerant due to having worked with a wide variety of cultures since he was 15.

Interestingly, although 81% of Nepali are Hindu and only 9% identify as Buddhists, Nepal holds a sacred place for both religions. The birthplace of Buddha is in Nepal, and in the mountain regions particularly the influence of Tibet – including many monks who have sought refuge in Nepal – means that the Himalayan region of Nepal is majority Buddhist. Hinduism and Buddhism are not seen as rivals in Nepal but merely variations on a similar religious history. In fact, it is not uncommon for both religions to worship at the same temples.

Case study: The Hunger Games

A finance company had been very stable in terms of employee turnover for many years, and a culture of intolerance had been allowed to embed itself. Those who were new to the organisation (especially those who were not of the male, pale and stale variety) were treated with obvious contempt. Aggression and name calling in meetings was commonplace, and it was openly voiced that there were too many women in the leadership team despite them only holding 40% of positions. Some board members still insisted on being referred to formally by the leadership team (for example, Mr Smith).

There were many long-serving middle-aged employees who had grown very comfortable and seemed oblivious to acceptable workplace behaviours, and believed they could do and say whatever they wanted without any repercussions. There was little desire to develop friendships in the group, and no time taken to consider other people's points of view before arguing with each other. Everyone was looking out for their own interests. In some instances, managers simply refused to do what the CEO asked of them just because they did not like it.

It was announced that the business was going to be restructured three months before anyone was advised how it would impact them individually. The employees were not used to change, and not knowing what the restructure would mean for them made them very uneasy. They could not confide in their colleagues because they were in competition with them if there were staff reductions; they were self-involved and running scared; they had no idea how to get another job and deep down likely knew the change would be very difficult. This resulted in people fighting each other for positions, spreading rumours and being aggressive towards the CEO and HR Director, resulting in a 'Hunger Games' situation.

Looking at the bigger picture and viewing the situation from the point of view of the business, being tolerant of others in a situation that was not pleasant for anyone would have made this experience bearable, but this was not the way they had been conditioned to behave. Predictably those who contributed most to the discontent in the team were given a redundancy and left kicking and screaming, with threats of legal action. The rest were left to pick up the pieces, create connection and tolerance, and build a culture that people wanted to work in, which could never have been achieved had the 'culture killers' been allowed to stay in the company.

Mantra:
WATCH YOUR BACK

If you find yourself in an 'outraged' culture
little can be achieved without removing
culture killers from the team.

CONNECTING THROUGH CURIOSITY

A sense of curiosity is invaluable when it comes to improving connection. In our lives today, my Sherpa has so many questions about the people he meets:

- How old are they?
- Where are they from?
- What sports do they like?
- Did they go to university?
- How much money do they earn?

- Who looks after their kids?
- When do they see their family?
- Why did they get divorced?

The frustrating part for me is that he often does not have the confidence to ask these questions of the person when he is sitting with them; he waits until we are in the car on the way home to ask me. *I'm sorry darling, I have no idea why he sold his house – why didn't you ask him?* The tricky thing is, in our culture some of these questions are not socially acceptable and he can't quite figure out which ones. He does not want to offend anyone, yet he craves that connection by getting to know their story.

When we ask open questions of others with genuine curiosity to learn more about them, we are creating a connection. High-performing teams have hundreds of such connections. Asking interesting and open questions shows you are interested to learn more about someone. Most people enjoy talking about themselves and sharing their story, you just need to be curious enough to ask.

An excellent way to build strong connection in teams is to have a one-minute share at the beginning of each meeting and ask a curious question. (You can download an editable meeting planner on my website: www.jadelee.com.au/resources.)

CONNECTION IS THE KEY TO RETENTION

For employees to be engaged, they need to feel connected to their team, the vision, the company and their work. When we enable that connection, it is similar to connecting a wire to a power source, allowing the electrons to flow, creating electricity. This electricity is the power that drives employee engagement and social connection in the team.

According to research by Ed Diener (aka Dr Happiness) and Shawn Achor (author of *The Happiness Advantage*), social connection is the factor with the greatest correlation to happiness in the workplace. Connection enables a supportive environment to help people thrive, happiness in the workplace to rise and productivity to soar. Not only are happier employees nicer to have around and easier to lead, they are also more productive.

When employees feel socially connected to each other they are unlikely to want to leave the organisation and retention improves. Often the only thing keeping an employee is 'the people I work with make me want to stay, I do not want to let them down'. In McKinsey research in 2021 one of the top reasons employees cited for leaving (or considering leaving) was that they lacked a sense of belonging at work (51%).

A common adage is that people do not leave companies, they leave managers. While it is ultimately up to the manager to address any problems within the team, often they are unable to improve a situation for a multitude of reasons, such as employment legislation and company politics. It's easy to simply 'blame the manager' when a problem arises, however in reality all team members are responsible for resolving team issues.

Trust is an aspect of a relationship that is earned through consistent and honest behaviour, and it can be lost very easily. People approach trust in different ways: some start new relationships with the expectation that you are trustworthy until proven otherwise, others can seemingly take years before they trust you. In the workplace we need to temper our approach for the different styles, but ultimately if we are looking to work in a collaborative and productive environment it is everyone's responsibility to build a reputation as a trustworthy team member. If you trust the people you work with you can endure whatever problems arise.

You do not have to like everyone you work with but you do need to trust them or the culture of the team breaks down. Trusting people to do their jobs and back you up when required is imperative to creating a strong team culture and in turn employee engagement. I trust my team has my back, and I have theirs. There are a few simple things you can do to gain and maintain trust in your team:

- do what you say you are going to do
- genuinely support your teammates without thought of personal gain
- do not gossip – if you gossip about anyone you could gossip about everyone.

A great team culture can flourish in the presence of a less-than-ideal leader if the employees trust each other and connect on a personal level. Employee happiness was found to be more closely correlated to the connections employees shared with their co-workers rather than those they shared with their direct supervisors by 23%, according to research reported in *The 5 Languages of Appreciation in the Workplace*. Trust is the building block of all relationships and should be high on the to-do list every day.

Authentic connections to the team, the vision and the organisation drive positive retention. In a team where these connections are strong, the bonds are harder to sever with more money or the promise of a promotion to leave the organisation. The connection is past the intellectual realm of *I love the work and the pay*; it is *I love the people, the environment and the support I get here*. Once you crack that emotional connection people genuinely want to stay in the team. That's the way of the Sherpa.

CONNECTION AND MENTAL WELLBEING

Connecting with colleagues is essential to work happiness. Research has shown that loneliness is as deadly as smoking 15 cigarettes per day, and people without healthy social relationships are 50% more likely to die prematurely. Establishing a true connection with each other results in having a supportive group of people. Try to remember to reach out to those people who may not realise how important social connection is.

A climbing party knows the value of connection to feel safe. They take the concept literally. When they are in a precarious situation or trekking with a tired team member, they physically tie ropes between each other. This method has helped the Sherpas get many people down from the summit of Everest safely.

The pandemic has highlighted that social connection is essential to our mental wellbeing. Perhaps the introverted people or those who are happy in their own space are the ones that we should be looking out for the most. They may not go out of their way to socialise outside of work, and the lack of connection outside a work setting takes its toll.

A good friend of mine is the most outgoing, loud, life-of-the-party person that you will ever meet. I still fondly remember a crazy night when she was creating a backstory for each of the models in a firefighters calendar with such witty humour and frivolity that everyone was laughing hysterically – this girl can captivate a room. So it was a shock to me to hear her say that she is an introvert. I was confused. 'You, an introvert?' I guffawed. 'Yeah!' she said. 'I always I assumed I was an extrovert too, but upon some reflection I realised I had just learnt extroverted behaviour from my twin sister when I was growing up. When I was funny and interacted animatedly with others, I got positive attention and concluded that this is the way I should behave.' This revelation got me to really thinking about the way we view introverts in our society and workplaces.

It is perhaps the most common unconscious bias we have in the recruitment process: that an extroverted person will be better for a job requiring a lot of communication with others, such as sales or leadership. While it has been shown that extroverts perform better in sales roles, this is not to say that introverts cannot have the skills to perform a sales role well and outperform an extroverted salesperson. Leadership studies have also shown that introverts are more effective leaders of proactive teams and are leaders who focus on the growth and support of their teams. Well-regarded introverted leaders include Barack Obama, Mahatma Gandhi and Michael Jordan. Who wouldn't like some of their leadership in their organisation?

We should also be conscious that those who are higher on the extroversion scale will commonly perform better and be more comfortable in an interview and in meetings. Therefore, it is easy to overlook the introvert as the best person for the job or the promotion. It is a common mistake though to put an introverted specialist into a leadership role without support. They may need training, specifically aimed at the skills they could enhance in undertaking the new role and becoming the best leader they can be. In a team setting, embracing the value that everyone brings even if they are not likely to speak up in meetings is essential.

According to Susan Cain, bestselling author of *Quiet: The power of introverts in a world that can't stop talking*, creating environments that encourage introverts and draw on their natural strengths will increase productivity, innovation and impact. By helping introverts to communicate, connect and lead in an authentic manner, we are also teaching managers to better engage with, and lead, their introverted employees. It's time to take a closer look at the role of introverts in organisations and learn how to allow them to reach their full potential for the benefit of the entire business.

It's a commonly held perception that extroverts must be better leaders. According to organisational psychologist Adam Grant's research, 96% of leaders and managers report being extroverted. And in a poll, 65% of senior executives said it was a liability for leaders to be introverted. Only 6% saw introversion as an advantage. We now know that the Sherpa leadership model is highly effective; supportive leaders who are focused on the development and wellbeing of their team are getting more from their people than can be achieved from the outdated directive style. It may just be that introverts are better suited to being the better leaders of the future.

GOOD COMMUNICATION DRIVES GOOD CONNECTION

In the modern workplace the variety of communication methods is seemingly endless: text, instant messaging apps, Zoom, MS Teams, various Google apps, email, phone and – dare I say it – 'face-to-face conversation'. When there are so many ways to communicate with your colleagues, it's important to remember that not all methods of communication are created equal. Some methods are of greater value in terms of creating strong connections, and in most cases these methods have a lower time cost.

We are increasingly relying on written communication, and the quicker the better. But the value of a text or instant message in developing and maintaining a connection with a colleague is basically zero, and this method can in fact have a detrimental effect on the relationship if care is not taken in the words chosen. We are actively leaning towards methods of communication that reduce connection between colleagues. In any given day we are bombarded with people having 'just a quick question' pinged onto our screen, and even the most disciplined of us will find that distracting – at best – or downright annoying. Receiving such a message while we are trying to deliver a report to a deadline or in the middle of something requiring attention to detail will affect our productivity.

A study at UCLA indicated that up to 93% of communication effectiveness is determined by nonverbal cues, indicating that face-to-face communication is of greater value than phone or written communication. Interestingly, face-to-face video link is considered by psychology associations to be equally valid for assessment and clinical evaluations. This can be considered reassuring in times when remote working is essential, or if you have a geographically dispersed team.

The perception is that it takes more time to talk than message, but the reality is often the act of conversing will enable all questions to be asked and answered in one sitting, as opposed to an email trail that can continue for days, miraculously adding more and more people to the tumbleweed, eating into an increasing list of employees' time and inbox capacity. Setting up a quick 10-minute meeting with someone in their diary will:

- ensure that they are present and ready for the meeting
- provide an opportunity for a quality conversation to increase social connection between colleagues.

In most cases this will be a lot more productive and meaningful than engaging in an instant message or email trail.

One of the reasons Sherpas form such great connections with the people they are trekking with is they spend days walking and sitting right next to them. Being able to see each other contributes greatly to forming strong bonds.

The table opposite shows how some of the most common workplace methods of communication affect our levels of connection.

The value derived from taking time to consider the needs of the other parties in a conversation is considerable. Engaging with someone when you are both fully present and focusing on the task at hand is a valuable endeavour and increases productivity.

We have all been in a meeting where others are discussing the impact of some communication that we have missed, frantically searching our emails during the meeting to figure out what the heck is being discussed ... *or was it in a group chat? ... where is this damn meeting agenda? Maybe that will give me some clue ... perhaps I was left off the email recipients?* When we finally summon up the courage to clarify, likely when we have been asked to weigh in with our opinion, we are told that it was in paragraph six of some organisation-wide communication, the title of which was so ambiguous that we didn't think it to be as important as the other 50 emails we had received overnight. *Honestly, why didn't someone just call me*, you think, exasperated. *This is going to have a massive impact on my project.*

Method	Focus	Connection
Scheduled face-to-face conversation while present	**THE RELATIONSHIP** – let's find a mutually agreeable time to work through this, show respect and improve our working relationship	♥ ♥ ♥ ♥ ♥
Unscheduled face-to-face conversation	**THE RELATIONSHIP** – let's develop an ongoing solution, suitable for all	♥ ♥ ♥ ♥
Scheduled voice call	**THE PROBLEM** – let's figure out how this happened	♥ ♥ ♥
Unscheduled voice call	**THE PROBLEM** – let's get it fixed NOW	♥ ♥
Group email	**YOU** – unsure how to get it fixed but someone on this email might know	♥
Text or instant message	**YOU** – your time is more important; it needs to be fixed	

A considerate colleague thinks about the impact on others as well as the desired outcome. Taking a little time to see the potential pitfalls of a chosen communication method will benefit everyone. When working remotely and flexibly the method of communication becomes even more important.

CONNECTION THROUGH LAUGHTER

A team who laughs together overcomes challenges together while keeping their humour. When a group of people share a laugh, this shows or perhaps initiates a connection between them. Humour is a powerful tool for connection; it is also a way to relieve stress, which let's face it never goes astray in the workplace. The good news is that in most workplaces, there are a multitude of things to keep us amused. You can just share the humorous anecdotes that we encounter regularly. Those OMG, face palm, FFS moments where you are exasperated that you are even living the situation.

Sometimes we need to suppress laughter for professionalism's sake, however there is no reason not to have a good belly laugh at the absurdity of a situation after the event. Sharing a laugh can bring people together even in the most trying of circumstances. Any debacle can be lessened by a giggle and embracing those around us to collaborate to find a solution rather than playing the blame game. When you embrace humour, you create connection and memories for a lifetime. I love a good laugh. I have a very distinctive laugh; it scares small children and I often get weird looks in public, but once people get to know me, they tell me they love it and think it contagious. Maybe they are just being nice because they think I might be embarrassed about it, but I embrace my crazy, scary, loud laugh because it makes me feel good – and perhaps because I cannot hear myself!

When we laugh, endorphins are released into the blood and dopamine is released into the brain. Endorphins help relieve pain and trigger feelings of pleasure; in fact, studies show that humans can endure 15% more pain by laughing for a few minutes before it is inflicted.

On the trek through Annapurna with my Sherpa after we had conquered Everest Base Camp, we had spent a full morning trekking, or I should say sliding over ice. It was bloody dangerous as I did not have crampons, and in certain places if you took a misstep and started sliding you would end up careering off a cliff. I had spent the morning oscillating between slipping and sliding and shuffling along on my bum. I was so frustrated and stressed that at one point I just sat down and cried after Gobinda told me it was another hour until the next town. I could not see how I could possibly make it another hour. We had not expected ice when we started off, and we were already an hour later than expected to be stopping for morning tea. I was hangry (so hungry you are angry) and completely overwhelmed by the seemingly monumental task ahead.

He looked at me with big smiling eyes and said, 'Do you need a rescue helicopter?' We had previously discussed the importance of having rescue helicopter insurance if you get injured on the mountain, and I had insurance up the wazoo as my mother had insisted on seeing the policy before I left Australia. Although I was pretty sure that emotional breakdown was not covered in the policy, and there was nowhere that a helicopter could safely get through the tree cover, I said, 'Yes, yes. Can you please go ahead and bring the rescue helicopter to me?'

We then started laughing at the absurdity of the situation. We sat there and laughed for a good 10 minutes. Another trekking group slid past us and concluded that we were complete loons, and that made me laugh even harder. I kept saying, 'I am staying here – you can go and get the rescue helicopter'. Eventually, I got up and continued. To my surprise and utter delight, the ice beneath our feet stopped within 100m of where I had my meltdown and I was at the next village with a Snickers and a hot chocolate in 20 minutes – those Sherpas need a better grasp on timeframes!

It is not about always seeing the bright side of life but accepting the setbacks and finding the humour. Having a laugh can improve your wellbeing and bring people together. Just be sure not to make light of a genuine disaster or laugh at someone else's expense.

Lessons from a Sherpa

- It is important to feel connected to the environment where you work. Be at one with the mountain; it helps you enjoy your day and be aware of risks.
- Connect with your teammates. Talk to each other. Sit down and look in each other's eyes. Get to know the people you are working with.
- The diversity of the team delivers the strength of the collective.
- Communication is key on the mountain. Share more than once and over-communicate if necessary.

- Communicate in different ways; words are not always the best way to convey a message.
- Have a laugh. It makes you feel good and relieves stress – every successful team has fun!

SIX

CONTRIBUTION

*'A group becomes a team when each member is
sure enough of himself and his contribution to praise
the skills of others.'*

Norman Shidle, author of *Clear Writing for Easy Reading*

As humans, it is in our nature to want to add value to the organisation that we work for. It is more than believing in a fair day's work for a fair day's pay, it is an intrinsic driver of human behaviour. When organisations create a productive environment where employees can perform to their potential, their employees contribute their best work. We need to ensure that the work someone is doing is adding value, and they are not just going through their day chopping down trees without taking the time to step back and sharpen the saw. Is their role enabling them to contribute in a meaningful way? Can they be productive and in turn be fulfilled in their work?

Sherpas believe they are making a significant impact on a team and on the lives of their clients every day. As well as keeping them safe, they are guiding them on a wonderful, once-in-a-lifetime experience. This contribution is a significant part of why they enjoy their work so much.

One definition of productivity can be doing things that we value (that is how I justify a yoga class as being productive), therefore it follows that productivity in a workplace is spending time on things that are going to provide value to the business and contribute to improvement. Answering the same question 50 times in a month and not taking the time to have it put on a SharePoint or intranet and emailing it out to the organisation is an example of being busy and not productive. This is also very frustrating. There is a native American parable where the chief asks, 'how long are we going to continue to fish the children out of the stream before we walk upstream and find out why they are falling in?'. Always work on the source of the problem people; it takes a bit of time, but the reward is being able to do more fulfilling work.

Interestingly, the converse is also true. Happy employees are also more productive and make more of a contribution. When they are in a good headspace, feeling valued, exercising, getting some downtime and treating themselves well they are going to contribute more meaningfully to the organisation.

'Productivity is vital when it comes to being happy. But don't confuse being productive with being busy. Simply adding more to do to your daily task list can create more stress and frustration in your life, making you miserable. Being busy means doing more and more things while being productive means doing something with purpose.'
Brian Tracy, world-renowned motivational speaker and time management expert

Sherpas don't busy themselves for the sake of it. When they are not trekking, preparing or cleaning up after meals or setting up camp they are doing very little. They know what they need to contribute to the team so specifically that once that is done, they are content to sit down with a cup of tea and relax.

It is helpful to ask yourself: is what I am doing accomplishing something? Am I creating an environment where my team can achieve or is the environment so reactive that we never get to work on the fulfilling projects? Carve out the time required to have the team work proactively and productively; engagement will improve and, in turn, the organisation will benefit.

CRAZY BUSY? MISTAKES ARE INEVITABLE

An under-resourced team is like a crack in the hull of a submarine; a tiny crack under pressure becomes a gaping hole which sinks the sub. Companies often try to cut costs by cutting labour; during downturns this is often prudent, however if we forget to upsize again when the business revenue and workload improves, we have a problem. If we expect that we can do more with less on an ongoing basis we are putting pressure on employees and creating a stressful environment.

When humans are stressed the chances of making an error increase significantly. Tolerance levels decrease and communication styles often become more direct. If we expect teams to work effectively when under-resourced for a prolonged period, we are setting them up for failure. It becomes a vortex that is difficult to escape. Employees become strained because they are overworked, they feel they cannot accomplish the tasks required, anxiety rises, they make a mistake, which leads to more stress – how can they fix it? Will they get in trouble? Will people say they are doing a bad job? – which creates more stress and leads to another mistake, which starts the cycle again. Eventually something must give, and either you have a workers compensation claim or a resignation on your hands. It is generally the best employees who get caught in this vortex because they care the most and are most concerned with doing a good job.

When workforce planning many organisations do not factor in employees being on leave. If you have a team of 10 people it is fair to say that someone will be on leave every day in the year if you allow four weeks' annual leave and five personal leave days, yet this is rarely considered when devising workforce plans. In most cases colleagues pick up the extra workload which places more weight on the team, or things are not actioned when someone is on leave, creating more pressure.

When a team is adequately resourced, they can support each other, make fewer mistakes and have time for a coffee and a laugh. They are more engaged and connected to their work. Consider flexible ways of resourcing the team; it might mean a part time or casual resource, planning leave differently, or looking at workload trends in recent years to be better prepared. Being proactive in resourcing the team will pay dividends long term, increasing retention of quality employees (after all, they are the most sought after from competitors).

Planning and adequate – or better yet slightly over – resourcing provides more time to employees to do their job well. They can also have a few minutes a day to connect to each other, have a chat at the watercooler and improve their social connection in the team. When something unexpected arises, the team can clear that hurdle with a smile because they have some capacity in reserve.

Learn from the Sherpas and allow your team enough time to have a cup of tea and a chat throughout the day because they have the skills and resources they need to do their job well.

RECOGNISING AND ADDRESSING ANXIETY IN THE TEAM

An intolerance of uncertainty is not only a trait of those who suffer from Generalised Anxiety Disorder (GAD); by nature, humans prefer certainty to uncertainty. We prefer to know where our next meal is coming from, that we have a roof to sleep under and – in a Sherpa's world – if the weather is going to enable a summit attempt when we have it planned.

Anxiety is increased by uncertainty; this is logical as anxiety is at its essence fear, and the fear of the unknown is the greatest fear of all. As leaders of teams, we acknowledge that there is much that is uncertain, but there is also a lot of certainty in our lives, jobs, teams, roles and organisations. People living with an anxiety disorder are prone to thinking the worst, imagining colleagues think they are not doing a good job, persistently questioning if they remembered to send that email, replaying conversations in their head to analyse if the other party was annoyed with them. We need to reassure our teams in any way we can about the things that we are certain of:

- ▲ 'What I know for sure is that there is a project milestone at the end of the month and we all need to contribute to ensure we meet it.'
- ▲ 'What I know for sure is we will need to closely monitor progress so we will be having a weekly meeting with mandatory attendance' (same time each week and do not change it).

- ▲ 'What I know for sure is we are the right team to be on this project and we have every faith that we will meet the deadline.'
- ▲ 'What I know for sure is that we will encounter obstacles, but if we all call them out early we will all support each other to overcome them.'

Communication is the enemy of uncertainty. Sherpas know this and are in constant communication on the mountain.

Our teams do not expect us to know everything, but they do expect us to show the way, be transparent and offer support. When teams are worrying about that which may never happen their focus deviates from what they are required to do. Communicate as much as you can to reduce uncertainty and keep the attention on contributing in a proactive way. A state of anxiety hamstrings a focused mind; anticipate that which may be worrying your team, communicate what you know for sure and reassure your team they have support.

Experience has shown me that many employers do not truly understand the effect that an employee suffering from anxiety has on the business bottom line. The root cause of the anxiety is irrelevant to the effect on their contribution to the business. Allow me to break this complex situation into words that are relevant to a manager or business owner. We have established that at its very core, anxiety is simply fear; it is often irrational fear but that doesn't matter to the 'lizard brain' as psychologists refer to it. I vividly recall my talented psychologist putting it into very easy terms for me to understand (forgive me Gillian for my paraphrasing but this is what I got out of it):

Our world has changed remarkably in the past 50 years. The pace, the constant stimulation, checking emails at all hours of the day, fear of switching off. Our brains have not had the time to evolve. Our brains cannot tell the difference between an email with unexpected news shocking us and a sabre-toothed tiger trying to attack us. The initial release of adrenaline to provide the energy to the body to get out of the situation and the subsequent release of cortisol to keep the body 'revved up and on high alert' is the same, and the body reacts in exactly the same way. When someone is in a state of anxiety their brains are screaming 'get me out of here!' and they find it difficult to calm down and focus on anything for too long.

An employee working with anxiety can easily be mistaken for someone who is not coping with the workload, is disorganised or is not 'cut out for the job'. Ironically it is the worker who takes the most pride in their work that may fall prey to this spiral. FOLO (Fear of Logging Off) is an actual thing. I was surprised to learn that it has a name, although I know many high performers who suffer from it. This is not something the peaceful Sherpas suffer from, and is another anxiety we in the Western world have inflicted upon ourselves.

Case study: A dedicated high performer

Roxanne was a well-respected worker who had been with the company for many years. She did a good job, was regularly praised and took pride in doing her work well. Then some things changed in her team: there was a new leader, communication deteriorated, and although she worked part time she had been expected to hold a full-time workload for over six months. Her workplace was going through a lot of changes and it was not only Roxanne who was becoming 'change weary'. In addition, the systems were clunky, there was a lot of manual intervention required and her boss did not take the time to understand the challenges of her everyday work. She was becoming more disillusioned with the work environment and her place in it. As time went on, she began to feel increased pressure from work and home and started making mistakes. Roxanne was a dedicated high performer and was not used to making mistakes, so this did not sit well with her. She became increasingly worried she was doing a poor job and started feeling disappointed that she was not offering the level of service she was used to. Things were getting missed. The colleagues around her understood the reasons for her mistakes and were understanding, but like all high performers the pressure she put on herself was higher than anyone else expected of her.

Over the course of a couple of months Roxanne asked for support but for one reason or another it was not forthcoming. Each individual thing she was facing was not a 'big issue' but when they were all combined she felt constantly overwhelmed, and the anxiety she was experiencing made it difficult for her to concentrate as her mind was racing and she could not work out where to start to get through all the work and also firefight the mistakes that were happening. At no point was her performance directly called into question by anyone other than herself, but she believed (rightly or not) that she was no longer up to the rigour of the job and she resigned.

The outcry from the business was resolute that she was an amazing worker and it was a devastating loss to the business. Roxanne was not the only person in the team who felt the way she did. It was inherent in the culture of that team that there was little support – everyone was expected to just get on and make things work despite the ever-changing landscape that they were working within. Roxanne had asked for help many times but because she was known as someone who could 'fix anything' and 'make stuff happen', there was no recognition given to how serious the situation was.

Mantra:
WATCH YOUR BACK

Look out for signs of disillusionment in high performers – if this is acted upon quickly by the team, the culture can improve. Hopefully the employee can be retained in the business.

It is usually the best employees or your highest performers who are at greatest risk of feeling anxious in the workplace. The reason is they really care (you are not going to find a narcissist worried about making a mistake) and they get more work because they are known as people who get things done. The old adage 'give it to a busy person and they will get it done' only holds true to a certain point; the busy person does have a breaking point. Although they can handle the stress and can get used to performing at the higher level of stress so it becomes normal for them, at some point they will break.

Busy people can believe that when their mind is racing and they are going a million miles an hour to get everything done it is just healthy stress, but more often than not this is anxiety. Once you get to the point that you don't know where to start, can't focus on what needs to be done and are unable to think through priorities, you are not present or focused on one task. This can look like you are disorganised, and this is what anxiety in the workplace looks like. There can be a stigma attached to anxiety, and those high performers do not want to be seen as weak (a common misconception about anxiety). In most instances these high performers might not even be aware that they are suffering from anxiety – it will remain undiagnosed because they will not want to admit that they have a problem. It is important to realise that it is not the individual who has the problem, it is in fact a symptom of the situation they find themselves in.

'Happiness inspires productivity.'

Shawn Achor, author of *The Happiness Advantage* and *Big Potential*

THE MODERN SABRE-TOOTHED TIGER

Email is an essential part of our workday, and it is difficult to imagine how companies can do without it (a few have tried and failed). Email is far too entrenched in our systems of work to remove entirely, however recognising the pressure that too many emails places on our colleagues, their productivity and ultimately our team culture is important. If employees allow emails to rule their day, their performance – along with mental health – can be severely affected. One in five people in Australia are working with a mental health condition, and this is significantly increasing, due in no small part to the expectation that we are 'available all the time'. Far too often, sending an email is seen as the quick fix to get an issue off one person's desk and make it another person's problem. This is not helpful to the individual receiving the email or the person wanting a solution to the problem that is being treated like a hot potato, or the productivity of the team or organisation.

In her book *Unsubscribe: How to kill email anxiety, avoid distractions, and get real work done*, Jocelyn Glei outlines the psychology behind why email is ruling our workdays and how to take back control. I have personally experienced the effect of email controlling my emotions when I was the victim of bullying in the workplace. I began to have a physiological reaction to receiving an email, and was checking my email far too frequently and fearing what I might find in my inbox. As part of my recovery, my psychologist explained to me that in highly stressful environments, receiving an email can feel akin to being attacked by a sabre-toothed tiger. The evolution of the digital age has happened amazingly quickly, and our brains are generations away from evolving to the extent required to cope in this digital age. Our brains cannot tell the difference between receiving an email from someone we perceive as attacking us and having a dangerous animal threatening to rip out our throats: the same fight-or-flight response is triggered by the amygdala and we are sent into the same hyper-vigilant state. Our lizard brain sees a confronting email as a genuine threat to life.

When the number or nature of emails gets to the point of having a detrimental impact on employees, the feeling of overwhelm can easily step into the realm of a mental condition. The fear and anxiety that is created is very real, and from our brain's perspective we are in perilous danger. This feeling is exacerbated if the culture of the organisation is to expect unrealistic turnaround on email activity and when there is no respect for holidays, time off or an 'out of office' message.

The impact of email on employees is a real problem in modern workplaces. It's important to create an environment where comfortable email management is achievable; creating 'email guidelines and expectations' within the team is a great idea. If the matter is so urgent that it needs to be responded to within 24 hours, should the recipient be contacted directly? Does this really require an email to get something actioned? Is it the best use of everyone's time to be cc'd on this email?

Years of working with high email traffic and in organisations where everything is urgent has enabled me to develop strategies for teams to reduce the overwhelm and increase connection in the workplace. Thinking about email as a tool, always ask yourself:

- Is this email adding a valuable contribution?
- Is there a better way to action what needs to be done?
- Does the email need to be sent now?
- Do I really need to cc others on this email?

THE IMPORTANCE OF CONTRIBUTION TO YOUR CUSTOMERS

At the heart of every business there is a customer, so it's likely that one of your aspirations will be around customer satisfaction. Your strategy of service delivery should hold that customer at the forefront of your mind. I recall being in a workshop many years ago and the question was asked, 'do you work in customer service?' Whether you like it or not, we *all* work in customer service. If you are not in a customer-facing role you are supporting those that are, and *they* are your customers. Provide good service to them and they can provide good service to the external customer.

The service or delivery model of an organisation needs to be aligned with what the organisation is aspiring to achieve.

The company strategy links the aspiration and delivery. If the aspiration is to be an employer of choice then it's important that the company has a strategy of paying in the high percentiles of market salaries, and offers flexible working and good employee benefits. High salaries alone will not attract the best people. There will need to be an investment in developing a good reputation in the market and treating good employees well so that they have more reason to stay than the salary. If the aspiration is to be a low-cost provider you will not be able to have the highest quality products and high rent offices and distribution centres.

It amazes me the amount of money some companies spend each year on attracting new customers when if they had treated the current ones better they would not need new customers. Get clear on your market and what you are offering your market. You cannot be all things to all people. Train your staff to over-deliver to that market to ensure repeat business and then build on that strong foundation. The key of course is having the right employees to execute your strategy. Each time I'm on hold in a call centre queue I wonder how much I can be valued as a customer if I have to queue, or worse still have to try to find the answer myself on a poorly designed website that astonishingly does not have a contact phone number.

Bernard Salt, one of Australia's leading social commentators of 'smashed avo' fame, wrote: ' ... saying you are customer focused while at the same time avoiding customer interactions are incompatible positions'.

Treat your employees well and they will exceed customer expectations. Think about what you want to achieve in your business and build the service delivery around that. Sherpas know that the best way to ensure success is for teams to stay focused – distractions are dangerous. Do not expect employees to go above and beyond every day but know that they will when they need to if they feel valued and appreciated.

ALLOW HIGH PERFORMANCE THROUGH GOOD TRAINING

Often employees are trained to an aspirational level and then when they get into the real job it is all thrown out the window and their immediate supervisor advises them to do something else. When writing training packages or training trainers it's important that they understand the inherent requirements of the role, including any time constraints that will be placed on the worker. If the expectation is that they are to do the job in a certain way but they are unable to do it in that way in the time allocated to them in a safe manner, this needs to be looked at.

I was reminded of this when my Sherpa started a job as a cleaner and he was trained to do detailed cleaning of surfaces. When he began working shifts his supervisor said there was no time to do detailed cleaning and he should just do spot cleaning. He was confused who he should listen to, and worried he would get into trouble if he did not do the tasks as he was trained. The company covered their own liability if anything goes wrong because they have 'trained employees' according to the correct procedure, but the employees are in cognitive dissonance ; they know they are supposed to do it in the way they were trained but the supervisor is telling them differently. This is exacerbated when companies rely on employees being trained by other companies and therefore there are a variety of perspectives on how the job should be completed.

McDonald's restaurants are often complimented for their intense training of all staff members – in fact, as a Registered Training Organisation they have been hailed as a training company not a hospitality company. It's one of the cornerstones to McDonald's success that anyone can walk into a McDonald's in Beijing, Paris or Chicago and the cheeseburger will be made the same with very similar ingredients – a traveller's 'safe haven'. (Interesting side note: there is no McDonald's in Kathmandu – insert shocked emoji – I assume because of the Hindu religion and the cow being sacred, as KFC is there and is always packed.)

Observing talent enter organisations over many years, I can attest that people who have worked at McDonald's for over 12 months are guaranteed to be able to follow systems, learn quickly and deliver according to deadlines. If they have cut the mustard with McDonald's, they will have the mantra of Quality, Service, Cleanliness and Value instilled in their being and will easily adapt to a new situation.

It's essential that we train employees as we expect them to perform the role. 'Oh, you should save the file there for audit purposes, but no one ever checks so I do not bother', is not acceptable. We need to have a clear understanding of how long a task should take and the correct way to do it. This likely means someone who is doing or has done the role to the level of quality required is the best person to teach a new starter.

What I have seen over the years is that employers would prefer to find an employee who can 'hit the ground running', which essentially means they have left training up to their competitors. Research by Peter Cappelli, director of the Wharton School's Center for Human Resources, has backed up this observation. Companies want workers they don't have to educate; in 1979, the average young worker received 2.5 weeks of training per year. By 1995, training time fell to just 11 hours, and by 2011 only a fifth of employees reported receiving on-the-job training from their employers over the past five years.

Well-trained workers are more productive workers, which means more productive teams and companies. When we take the time to train our employees in how we expect a task to be completed, we ensure they are doing it the most efficient way for our company. Do not rely on the training of other companies as every company is different and every employee learns in a different manner. Train them as you would expect them to do the role – do not train them in a 'perfect world' process if no one in the organisation has time for or is following that process. Be fair to the employee and set them up for success.

FEEL THE FEAR AND DO IT ANYWAY

When faced with any change it is natural to be worried. It's the body's way of protecting us from the unknown. However, if we stay stagnant and do not challenge our fears then we are not giving ourselves the best chance in this amazing life. Over 80% of Australians are not engaged in their work – that is a staggering majority of us who are getting up each morning feeling indifferent at best or devastated at worst about the prospect of going to work. This makes me sad to my core. I see it in people's eyes as they trudge into their high-rise buildings wishing they had a role they were passionate about, where they believed they were making a difference, or maybe that their lotto numbers would come up. We would be kidding ourselves if we thought we had not been there at some point (even if only for a day); for some of us that feeling of disengagement is enough to make a change but for others our fear holds us back.

Allowing fear to rule our decisions becomes problematic. In her book *The Loudest Guest: How to change and control your relationship with fear*, Dr Amy Silver talks about the different roles we can allow fear to have in our lives. She writes we should welcome fear but not allow it to control us, just give it the authority to provide commentary, which we can take on board and then make our own decisions. Fear is a useful emotion; it protects us from danger, and through the ages it has helped us survive when being approached by a sabre-toothed tiger. We should however recognise that some of our fears – such as public speaking or going for a job interview – are unlikely to actually kill us, yet the same fear response is felt biologically. Being aware that the fear response works the same if we are triggered by a public appearance or a cougar is helpful to put our fear in perspective.

I have given a lot of thought to why people resist a career change far beyond a time when the contribution they are making is not fulfilling them. We need to feel that we are making a solid contribution to be engaged in our work. In the Himalayas there are few choices or options for the Sherpas but they remain happy. Workers in modern workplaces look at things differently.

When you know you have choices but feel trapped and unable to make a move there are three aspects that need to be addressed, as outlined overleaf.

Overcoming fear of change

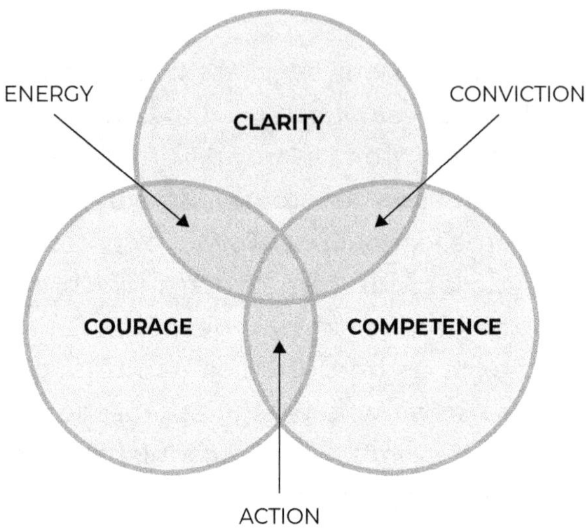

You must have the courage to make a change and strong clarity about where you want to get to. This provides the energy for you to start the change. When you believe you have the competence to do the role and the clarity of why you want to do it you have the conviction in your ability to get there. Conviction is vitally important in making a career change because it's what shows others you believe in yourself and have the confidence to face any challenge presented and be successful.

When you combine courage with competence you can act. You are not being held back by fear and you will have overcome the tendency to stay stagnant with the passion you have for what lies beyond the change.

In life you are a sum of your experiences. If you are happy with your experiences being similar throughout your life, if you were lucky enough to have found your dream job out of university, if your risk profile is such that making a change would be a terrible experience, if you honestly love the people you work with and are excited by the prospect of going to work each day, then by all means stay in that great job. But if you are only there because you are scared to make a move, it is time to figure out why you are fearful, get clarity on what you do want and curate the energy to make a change.

Lessons from a Sherpa

- Ask yourself, is what you are doing adding value? If not, find a way to contribute.
- Know what your role is and how your contribution is helping the team. It will keep you motivated.
- The best thing to ensure success is to stay focused – distractions are dangerous.
- Train people in the way they need to do the work. Train them well enough that they know how to get themselves out of trouble.
- Contributing is a choice. If you don't contribute, even if the team summits it will be a hollow success.

SEVEN

COLLABORATION

'I don't necessarily have to like my players and associates but as their leader I must love them. Love is loyalty, love is teamwork, love respects the dignity of the individual. This is the strength of any organization.'

Vince Lombardi, former American football coach

Creating an environment where each individual's contribution is recognised and organised into a collaborative outcome is the role of the Sherpa leader. We need to ensure that everyone has their role to play, and that efforts are not being duplicated. This is especially true on the mountain when communication in the moment can be difficult. Every ounce of energy is precious, so a well-oiled machine of team collaboration is essential to success.

There are a variety of factors that encourage a team to work effectively together and produce excellent results. These are mainly related to creating a positive team culture where people feel safe to contribute and valued for what they offer.

APPRECIATION IS PRICELESS

Preparing cups of tea for the team: $100

Risking your life to install ladders and ropes: $1000

Trekking through the night to support someone to summit: $100,000

Receiving a heartfelt thank you and a tip at the end of the trek: Priceless

On the second day of my trek to Base Camp, my Sherpa told me the story of how he once rescued a trekker who was suffering from altitude sickness. She had become sick in the afternoon and evening and had a headache and was vomiting. These are typical symptoms of altitude sickness, and the only cure – and what is essential to avoid death – is to descend. She was unable to walk by herself and the helicopters cannot safely fly at night, so my Sherpa and another one carried her down the mountain in the middle of the night. By all accounts she was an overweight lady, making the task more challenging. When I heard this story, I thought they certainly went above and beyond the call of duty, especially when I learned that her boyfriend was unable or unwilling to assist. The Sherpas carried her through the night and got her low enough that the symptoms subsided.

Knowing how little they earned in comparison to Westerners, I asked if he received any tips from her. 'Yes,' I was told, 'she gave us very good tips, and was very grateful for us helping her.' They had stayed in contact, and she had offered to have them visit her in the UK, which I thought was a heartfelt display of appreciation and was certainly in part why my Sherpa spoke about her with fondness.

Those who provide the most value in teams will contribute the discretionary effort with little thought. They do it to reinforce (mainly to themselves) that they are doing a good job. They take pride in their work and derive a feeling of being valued from performing a role to the best of their ability. These are the employees who rarely complain, get on with their jobs and work hard. These employees have a can-do attitude and are often the busiest people in the department. They can answer all the questions and know the best way to get anything completed. Because of their friendly and helpful attitude, they are often taken for granted in the workplace and potentially end up with more than their fair share of work. It is appropriate that the team should be saying thank you and recognising them in a way they will appreciate.

In their book *The 5 Languages of Appreciation in the Workplace*, Gary Chapman and Paul White discuss the five different ways we can show appreciation in the workplace:

1 *Words of affirmation:* Saying or writing a note to people to encourage them to feel good about themselves. 'Nice work', 'great job on that' or even a simple 'thank you'.
2 *Acts of service:* Helping colleagues by doing some work for them, offering to help out with something, or simply communicating when you are doing a task that you might be able to train them in.
3 *Receiving gifts:* People like receiving presents. Often an unexpected present regardless of its value will be greatly appreciated. Also presents to recognise employment milestones or bonuses that reflect the work fall into this category.

4   *Quality time:* Giving someone your undivided attention is very special. Having lunch or an uninterrupted meeting with the boss is very valuable to many team members.
5   *Physical touch:* This needs to be appropriate for the workplace – a high five or a handshake (or an elbow bump when socially distancing) would be the safest options.

Many companies have an employee recognition program in place. This can be a helpful initiative – but it will not in itself create a supportive culture. It's a tool that can be used in developing a culture of recognition and appreciation. A common downfall of employee recognition programs is they miss the vital point of ensuring the recognition is delivered in a way the individual will appreciate. The best recognition programs allow latitude in the reward and the delivery. Some employees will love a morning tea in their honour where they are the centre of attention (quality time), whereas an introverted employee may prefer a card and a voucher to a 'discretionary day off' (receiving gifts). The key is to model an appreciative and grateful approach and encourage others to do the same.

We should never underestimate the value of a heartfelt 'thank you'. Chapman and White's research showed that 79% of employees who quit their jobs voluntarily cite not feeling appreciated as a key factor in leaving. When employees have their contribution recognised, they are more likely to continue with the discretionary effort. In addition, according to the 2021 Culture Report from Achievers, those who were recognised for their achievements in the last week were 4.5 times more likely to feel a strong sense of belonging to the team and the organisation than those who were not.

When we have a team of people working together appreciating each other and contributing discretionary effort, we have a supportive and engaged team who are more productive, happier and simply more fun to be around. That's the way of the Sherpa.

COURAGE PRECEDES SAFETY

I put it to you that although most employees believe they will have the courage to speak up if they feel safe, the truth is that courage precedes safety. When we have the courage to give feedback, point out a risk or call out the elephant in the room, that enhances the psychological safety in the group and encourages others to do the same, thus creating a psychologically safe environment.

We are often scared to point things out or ask a question, believing that we should know the answer (*I must have missed that email – I'll check when I get back to my desk*), but this is often the question that everyone else in the room is scratching their head about too. The same can be said for giving a colleague some feedback: *surely they must have heard this before? I am not putting my neck on the chopping block if they respond negatively to the feedback.* There are remarkably few people who have the courage to speak up in workplaces (particularly to those in authority) and therefore it is quite possible that what might appear to be obvious feedback has never been passed on to the individual.

Case study: Past the point where he could ask for help

I was coaching an executive on his interview skills. He had a large team and had been recruiting employees for at least 25 years. Although he was really personable and made the candidates feel at ease, he had a tendency to answer the questions for the candidate and clearly had an unconscious bias towards certain candidates. *Surely, he has been trained,* I thought, *surely he knows the candidate is required to answer the questions, surely he knows the difference between a leading question and an open question? Does he even know what behavioural interviewing is?* I found myself wondering.

Time to put on my superhero suit and take a few deep breaths. I started by asking some general questions, and acknowledged that interviewing can be a difficult skill to learn and after doing it for 20 years I still stuff up sometimes. I pointed out the positives of what he was doing but also made it clear there were areas where he could improve, and I was sure to approach it with a joking and light manner. It was scary to be honest; he was in a position of authority and I was not convinced he would take the feedback well. During the conversation I learnt that he had never had interview training and he had no idea what unconscious bias meant. He was likely to favour someone with a similar educational background to him and did not realise he answered as well as asked some questions. He was eager to learn how to improve. Because I had the courage to address the situation, he felt safe enough to ask for help and now regularly confides in me when he is unsure of something in my area of expertise.

Mantra:
SHOW ME THE WAY

When team members feel safe enough to
be vulnerable it creates an opportunity
for improvement.

The work of Dr Amy Edmondson, author of *The Fearless Organization* and an expert in psychological safety in organisations, backs up my observations. She says that to step up to the learning zone we need to feel psychologically safe. The executive referenced in the case study was likely sitting in the anxiety zone when it came to interviews. He had never been trained but it had gone past the point where he could ask for help without appearing incompetent, so he was just going through the motions the best he knew how, afraid of being found out as a fraud.

When we feel safe to ask for help and speak our truth and are driven to achieve team goals we are learning, growing and collaborating as a team. The following safety success model shows the relationship between the two, and what results if teams are not influenced to work towards the vision and feel safe to be their authentic self.

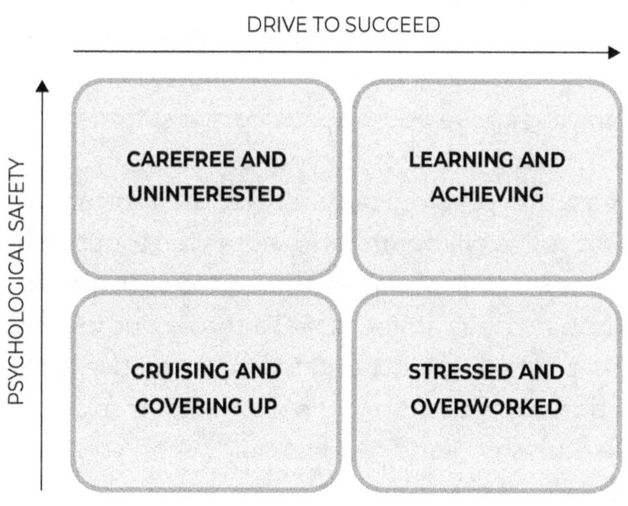

In Dr Edmondson's TED Talk she relays three things that we can do to create a psychologically safe environment:

- *Frame the work as a learning:* If you are looking at a mistake that has been made, approach it as a 'lessons learned' exercise.
- *Acknowledge your own fallibility:* It is easier for people to be vulnerable when they are reminded that everyone has faults.
- *Model curiosity:* Ask a lot of questions; it encourages people to reveal more and hide less information.

In my experience when we feel the need to be courageous it is because we crave the safety on the other side. If I have the courage to kill the snake, I will then be safe; if I have the courage to fight against evil then peace will be restored; if I have the courage to tell my fellow Sherpa that they are performing an unsafe act on the mountain then all in the vicinity will be safe. As is often the case, the way the message is delivered is the difference between success and failure. The above tips will assist in having those courageous conversations and improving the psychological safety in your team.

The reason psychological safety is so important is that the best way to fully collaborate and work well together is to garner everyone's views. To have a thriving, creative environment, team members need to feel safe to throw out ideas that may not be great but will initiate and feed the creative process. True collaboration comes when you have free communication, can ask anyone anything and request help when you need it. True collaboration is knowing that no one will get there unless everybody gets there.

SELF-AWARENESS AND APPROACHABILITY

True collaboration comes when all team members feel comfortable to approach anyone else to ask for help, guidance or an opinion. Managers often brag that their door is always open but, in my experience, there are very few managers who live by this premise. In many cases they do not have the time, or do not make the time, to really listen to the concerns of their people. We know that to have a culture of continuous improvement we need to have employees who are comfortable to address aspects of their work that can be improved, however unless we have managers who are actively working on being approachable this may not happen. With the growth in remote working this is set to become more of an issue as employees may need to go out of their way to have time with their boss and raise any concerns.

Samuel Goldwyn, a former Hollywood movie director, was famously quoted, 'I don't want any yes men around me, I want everyone to speak up even if it costs them their job'. Unfortunately, it may well be that employees risk their job by speaking up and advising on areas of improvement. This is often due to a lack of self-awareness in the management team. When executives spruik that they want employees to speak up, question and offer suggestions, they may not realise that the middle managers below them do not have the skills to handle constructive feedback or the self-awareness to accept feedback that they may not agree with. It is important that employees feel comfortable to bring forward ideas, but the approachability of managers goes a long way to ensuring that this happens. Megan Reitz, co-author of *Speak Up*, stresses that we 'simply do not realise how risky it can feel for others to speak up'.

This can be especially true in a Sherpa's world. The people leading the expeditions can be big personalities with a clear drive for excellence. Culturally it's difficult for a Sherpa to raise concerns with someone like that. They know this person is between them and a much-needed paycheque at the end of the trekking season. If an expedition leader is a direct communicator, someone who is driven to get things done and more task than people orientated, they may not be seen as approachable to the Sherpas. The irony is they may *think* they are approachable as they have either not been given the feedback that they are 'scary' or have dismissed said feedback without doing the self-reflection to determine if there is any truth in it. The key to developing self-awareness is asking questions of those around you in an open and transparent way. This will only bring insight if you are willing to accept what they tell you. Tasha Eurich, organisational psychologist, researcher and author of *Insight: The power of self-awareness in a self-deluded world*, conducted research in conjunction with *Harvard Business Review* which found that 95% of people think they are self-aware but only 10% to 15% actually are. This statistic is horrifying when you think about it, but was not a great surprise to me given my experience with the corporate world.

The key takeaway from this research is that most of us need to make a concerted effort to be approachable. If we are seen as unapproachable, working on our self-awareness will improve this. The perception of approachability will likely decrease with the level of stress that we are under, as most people revert to a more directive communication style when under pressure. Smile more, ensure that you have time for people when you have meetings booked in, be present in conversations and listen to your team's concerns; it is where the gold for continuous improvement lies. Walk the talk. Your door doesn't have to always be open but when it is, welcome people, listen and seek clarity. Take the time to consider how you can be more available to people working remotely. A drop-in hour twice a week might work, but often scheduling one-on-one and team meetings and regarding these meetings as non-negotiable calendar entries can be enough.

Feedback is an opportunity to improve, but only if we have the courage to self-reflect and try to increase our emotional intelligence. It is not easy, but it is worth making the effort as self-awareness is essential for any good leader to become great, whether you are leading yourself, your team, your household or your organisation.

It is often the case that we only know a minuscule amount of the skills that a teammate has developed over the course of their lifetime. As we get to know them better and listen to what they are saying – really listen, with the intent to understand and not just respond – we may discover other areas where we are able to learn or receive support from this teammate. It may also reveal areas where you can contribute further to the team using your unknown skills.

POINTING OUT MISTAKES IS EASY – MAKE A POINT OF GIVING POSITIVE FEEDBACK TOO

Have you ever read and reread an email 10 times before hitting *send* – hoping that you have not put a comma in the wrong place, missed a capital letter, referenced someone incorrectly or overstepped the mark in the wording? You finally hit *send* and as it is leaving your inbox, you notice one minor detail that is not right and start obsessing over it. When that one 'well meaning' person points out the error, you are ashamed: *everyone thinks I have no attention to detail, I should have checked it again.* Interestingly, you are likely to have received many compliments about your work from colleagues previously, but it doesn't make it any easier to deal with the error and you have likely forgotten that anyone has given you positive feedback in the past.

I have given this phenomenon some thought, and I have come to two conclusions:

- It's much easier to find fault with someone's work than to compliment it.
- We take a disproportionate amount of offence to negative feedback than we feel encouraged by positive feedback.

There is a marvellous invention called a fault finder which is extremely useful to electricians; it enables them to quickly resolve where an electrical circuit has been cut. What is so beneficial about this tool is that it is dealing with wires. Wires do not have feelings; they do not care if they have made a mistake by losing contact with their opposite wire buddy. We need to be more thoughtful when we are dealing with beings of the human variety, those with feelings, expectations of themselves and a drive to do a good job. They do not appreciate the fault finder quite as much.

It can be helpful to think about the motivation behind pointing out the error, but it is more than that; we need to foster a culture where people embrace mistakes and feel safe in the knowledge that making mistakes or encountering failure simply means they are on the road to improvement. When a team member is fearful of making a mistake, they will not contribute new ideas or strive to learn new things. When we are learning we will always make mistakes. The only way to be sure not to make a mistake is to stop growing, and this is not a way to improve team performance.

Storytelling when pointing out a mistake can be invaluable; it shows your authenticity, vulnerability and compassion all at once. This is assuming of course you are telling a vulnerable tale of when you made a cringe-worthy mistake, not one of being infallible! When the team has psychological safety they feel safe being wrong or different, they will be more creative, contribute more fully and think laterally to problem solve. When you have the right people in your team, simply pointing out the error will be enough; they will be mortified that the error has occurred and will likely be one step ahead of you to work out how to fix it.

CREATE A CARING CULTURE

Have you ever rolled your eyes at someone who talks about their 'work husband' or 'work wife' – how silly and unprofessional, right? Well perhaps not; 2020 research from the Wellbeing Lab shows that when employees have close personal relationships at work their wellbeing improves. There is evidence for creating and supporting stronger, more meaningful relationships at work to improve employee engagement.

When there is a close personal relationship, it's easier to share more private thoughts and to recognise if something is not right. It may be a caring ear or a shoulder to cry on when something goes wrong. Having those strong relationships at work reassures people they are not in this alone and so they feel supported.

Check in with those around you; lead with, 'Are you okay?' – but don't just leave it there. If you sense that there is something wrong, there probably is. If they really don't want to tell you, they won't, but you can leave them with a feeling that they can come back to you at some point if they need to. Don't ever feel silly for making your concerns known: the person you are worried about may not have the mental capacity to make that decision themselves. Perhaps they are fine, but we want to create a caring culture where people are comfortable and trust each other enough to say if they are not.

It's easy to forget that there are a lot of people who are high functioning that are suffering with a mental illness. They are the ones who are often most at risk because they think that nothing serious will happen, but they may be living one issue away from falling apart. We can all seek out relationships at work that can support us, and try to ensure that others in the team do the same. It is human nature to connect better with some people more than others, however we should try to 'get along' with everyone to show we are committed to the culture (and for less angst in our day).

The 'inspirational teams' we want to emulate in the cor-porate world must rely on one another in life-and-death situations (a mountaineering team, armed services teams or a yachting crew) – they know they have each other's backs when the chips are down. High-performing athletic teams have the weight of the world on their shoulders and come together at the precise moment needed to score and win the game. Their relationships are strong. They are also an example that you do not have to like someone to have a strong relationship with them. What are the chances of connecting strongly with all of the other 20 people in the football team? But they still develop trust and empathy with each other and know they are supported.

CULTIVATE CALMNESS

My Sherpa is the calmest person I know. If you want an argument, which I never do, he is not the man to try to antagonise – it simply will not happen. There was an instance where someone literally stole his Hungry Jack's takeaway from him in a lunchroom and he just let her have it because she said she was hungry. No questions asked, he just wandered back to Hungry Jack's and ordered some more.

I suffer from anxiety, and by my own admission get cranky at him and overreact about things that are not even close to his fault. When I'm being particularly cranky with him, Gobinda looks at me and says, 'how long since you've been to yoga meditation?'. He calls it 'yoga meditation'. In the Western world 'yoga' is generally the physical poses and 'meditation' is about calming your thoughts. In Nepal it seems that this is regarded as the same thing, which in fact it should be. Hence Gobinda's term 'yoga meditation'.

I find it in endearing that my husband takes this approach – most men would yell at me, questioning why I was being so painful and cranky, causing me further agitation. I would get my back up and make it his issue, resulting in a day of drama. Gobinda's spin puts the onus back on me to calm my mind and not take it out on him. I have to say that it does work, because he shows that he is concerned about me and is genuinely perplexed as to why I am behaving in a manner that to him is irrational ... okay, okay ... so it is irrational! Damn anxiety!

I tell this story to convey two points:

▲ Self-care is the last thing that should be dropped when you are feeling stressed. Nearly all of us let positive habits drop when workload increases, but when we feel stress rising then more than any other time we need to:
- guard our sleep like gold
- eat well and get our daily vitamins
- limit alcohol consumption
- make exercise a priority
- maintain any stress-management strategies.

▲ Coming from a place of genuine compassion can defuse even the most volatile situations. When we feel attacked it is natural to become defensive, but if we can remove ourselves from taking it personally and try to see another point of view we will likely get an amicable outcome. Recognise that there may be other factors at play and the behaviour may have nothing to do with us.

The evidence of the positive effects that yoga has on wellbeing is far more than anecdotal. There are many papers that provide scientific evidence of improvements in wellbeing, including significant improvements in anxiety, depression, fatigue, headaches and overall physical fitness. How long since you have put your mental health as your top priority? It's amazing how things seem to be easier when we do.

When we are in a calmer frame of mind, less distracted and focused on one thing, we can collaborate more effectively with our colleagues. How often do you sit down with other people completely dedicated to the task at hand? When we are multi-tasking we lose our focus. It seems obvious, so why do we continue to do it? Because it is the expectation of the corporate workplace. But 10 minutes of meditation before sitting down to work will set you up for 40 minutes of focused work, and you will certainly produce better work and save time in the long run.

Staying focused on the mountain is literally a matter of life and death for the Sherpa. On a mountainside, every step requires focus. If we gave it a higher priority in our workdays we could slow down, have less mental illness, higher quality work and better outcomes. Slow down to get there safely.

MOTIVATION TO COLLABORATE

When striving to create a culture of support, true collaboration and high performance, we can reflect on the methods we use to motivate. Striking a balance between intrinsic and extrinsic motivation is useful. In a culture where there is internal joy in the work that is done or the outcome rather than what employees can receive for doing the work, it is easier to maintain levels of motivation. However, we must recognise that often people are performing a role they may not be intrinsically motivated by – or at least not all aspects of the role – and this is where extrinsic motivation comes in.

When intrinsically motivated you perform an act for the joy of it; the act is rewarding in itself. However, when you are extrinsically motivated you do it to earn a reward or avoid a punishment.

A civil engineer may be intrinsically motivated because they love the work of designing bridges and they know that designing the bridge in the Philippines will result in a village not being cut off from supplies for three months of the year. They are doing good work. In addition, they know that if they get the design finished by the project deadline, they will also receive extrinsic motivation in the form of a monetary bonus in their annual review. The village gets the bridge before the monsoon season, the individual gets a bonus and the company builds a reputation for being reliable at delivering projects. This is the triad of success: the client is satisfied, the employee is engaged and the company is profitable.

In her book *Mindset*, Carol Dweck highlights that people with a growth mindset find their work meaningful because they are applying themselves, giving their best and solving challenging and important problems. These people are intrinsically motivated by the desire to learn and improve, to find meaning and to serve a cause.

People who are extrinsically motivated rarely improve the culture of a workplace. Once their basic needs are met there is little more to be gained from them in terms of improving how the team relate to each other. In a sales team they may be motivated by the bonus and that will get them to put in the extra effort, but it will not encourage them to support their colleagues, pass on a lead or try to motivate other people, which are traits of a culture that people want to work in. If they are intrinsically motivated to feel good by supporting others, enjoy motivating a team or just love the thrill of meeting targets then, although the bonus structure is there, it is not their main driver.

A knowledge of how intrinsic and extrinsic motivation works can assist us when determining how people are inspired and why they may behave in a certain way. This is helpful to know as a leader to ensure that you are motivating the individuals in your team in a way that is going to get the best outcome and improve collaboration. Structuring a team so they are in the main intrinsically motivated will go a long way to creating a positive team culture.

As we have seen, Sherpas are intrinsically motivated because they don't separate work and life. They love being in the mountains and they love helping people; that they get to enjoy these things at work is a bonus most Western workers miss out on. Of course there will be parts of their job they do not enjoy, but not enough to affect their overall satisfaction with what they do.

Treating people justly also plays an important role in developing an engaged team. We have outlined that one of the key components of a positive workplace culture is trust. Leaders are in a privileged position to ensure their employees are being fairly remunerated for their skills, experience and contribution to the business. According to Herzberg's two-factor theory of motivation, salary is a 'hygiene factor', meaning if you are not being paid a competitive salary it causes dissatisfaction. Recognition and status are motivation factors – getting a pay rise or promotion to recognise the improvement you have made through the year will increase your motivation.

In effect, if an organisation pays fairly and recognises the contribution of everyone, it will have employees who are motivated by the two factors. Conversely, if an employee knows (or strongly suspects) that they are not receiving a fair salary in comparison to their counterparts it will affect their feeling of being valued (status), reduce motivation and cause friction in the team, potentially resulting in devastating consequences for employee and team engagement if not addressed.

These are three actions that should be avoided to have a team of fairly remunerated, engaged and productive employees:

- *Rewarding the squeaky wheel.* The saying, the squeaky wheel gets the oil, is all too often the case when it comes to salary negotiation: the employees who complain and threaten to resign are those who are rewarded with a salary increase to retain them. This is sending the wrong message to the team: if you contribute in a negative way to team cohesion by complaining and being disengaged you will get a pay rise. The employees who get on with the work, help each other and do not complain are being disadvantaged.

▲ *Relying on a contract clause to enforce employee behaviour.* 'But my team are not allowed to discuss their salary'... seriously ... if you believe that will stop them, you are probably looking out the window at a flock of flying swine. Relying on a clause in a contract to mitigate an issue created by unfair management is abdication of responsibility by a fair leader. A far better approach is to have a team who are remunerated in parity with their peers, recognising different levels of contribution. A fair evaluation, recognising effort and improvement goes a long way to developing an engaged team.

▲ *Dangling the golden carrot.* When recruiting, establish early in the attraction process what maximum salary you can offer someone, considering the market and salary parity in the organisation. If a candidate is not willing to consider the salary determined, do not take them through to interview: it will only end in disappointment for everyone. If it becomes clear during the process that the determined salary will not attract a suitable candidate and it needs to be increased, ensure this is flagged to be addressed at the next remuneration review to ensure parity. In this instance the recruitment process revealed the current employees are worth more in the market and this needs to be recognised for retention.

According to Salary.com's 2021 Pay Practices and Compensation Strategy survey, 69% of organisations do not believe their employees were paid fairly. Having held roles across a variety of industries and been privy to salaries of staff from entry level to CEO, I can assure you that salary disparity among colleagues is a real problem in our workplaces and does, without doubt, contribute to disconnection in teams. Coaching on how to remedy the situation has at times been challenging, but it is everyone's role to take responsibility when we become aware of such disparities. Do not just look at the numbers; look at the story behind the individuals, and critically and without bias evaluate fairness in salaries. Not only will it improve trust in your leadership and display that the organisation is serious about living their values, but it is also the right thing to do.

CULTURE KILLERS SLAY COLLABORATION

'Nothing will kill a great employee faster than watching you tolerate a bad one!'

Perry Belcher, marketing strategist

A culture killer is someone who, for whatever reason, does not live the values that are instilled (or are attempting to be instilled) in the team and purposely goes about breaking down the glue that holds the team together. A culture killer can be a long-standing team member or someone you bring into the team. The latter is generally easier to identify, as over time we become used to the behaviour of the entrenched culture killers and have worked out ways to deal with them.

All too often managers are willing to bring a new employee into the team because of their amazing technical ability and conveniently ignore the behaviours they exhibit through the hiring process and probation period. A positive team culture is like a gold bar; you work hard to attain it and then put it in a safe to ensure that no one will take it away. Be incredibly careful who has access to your gold culture, as once it's gone you not only have to start from scratch you must win back the trust that has been lost within the team. However, as already outlined, the culture will ebb and flow with the personalities in the team and situations – no matter how hard we try, we cannot lock up the culture. We need to be vigilant to observe any changes and address things that are causing the culture to fluctuate

A 2015 report 'Toxic Employees in the Workplace' found that good employees are 54% more likely to quit when they work with a toxic employee. In addition, they found extremely strong evidence suggesting that toxic behaviour is contagious. Employees are many times more likely to engage in toxic behaviour if they are exposed to other toxic employees.

The technical ability of a climber is something that should be considered when bringing them onto an expedition team, but their behaviour is even more important. If they have selfish or undisciplined behaviour and the leader is unable or unwilling to address it, it will cause disharmony in the team. The last thing you need when you are on the mountain is a rogue team member who believes their summit attempt is more important than that of the team. It is essential that everyone trusts each other and can collaborate well for a trek to be successful. When teammates do not want to work with a toxic colleague, collaboration will quickly disappear.

THE EFFECT OF HIERARCHY ON COLLABORATION

When I first transitioned to an internal human resources role, I quickly found the value of an organisational chart. It was my secret weapon to determine all manner of information about an organisation that may not be apparent without a quick look at an 'Organogram' as the South Africans call it. A picture paints 1000 words as they say, and an organogram is perhaps the best example of this. It relays so much about the way that an organisation operates.

The height of the hierarchy can explain a lot about the way the organisation will work, as discussed in the research paper 'Analytical Comparison of Flat and Vertical Organizational Structures'. Flat organisations have relatively few layers or just one layer of management. This means that the 'chain of command' from top to bottom is short and the 'span of control' is wide. Practically, this means that there is generally better communication and ability to be adaptable, and decisions are made through discussion and are quicker to be made as generally fewer people need to be involved.

The converse is also true; the more layers that are added to an organisation the slower decisions are made. It is easier for employees to get lost, and very often employee engagement scores are lower as they feel that they are a lot further away from the decision makers. One step any organisation can do to start improving the clarity for employees and quicken the decision-making is to get very clear of the organisational structure, and don't keep it a secret. An organisational chart is an aid for all employees to understand the business and how to get things done and should be available to all and regularly updated. It is also vital to maintaining an accurate workforce plan and budget.

When developing working teams, they are best structured with little or no hierarchy. Simple two-layer structures of leader and team members is the best way to support collaboration, keep the lines of communication open and increase connection with the group. Indeed, teams that can operate with only members with leadership qualities are most effective at collaborating as each team member has the anonymity to keep them on track and offer suggestions and support.

On the mountain, the teams that work the best have reduced hierarchy. Everyone's opinion is recognised and valued. To be safe at high altitude the person with the best cognitive ability at the time (the people not as affected by the high altitude) should be listened to, regardless of whether they are the newest member of the team or the owner of the expedition company. During the 1996 Everest disaster, expedition leader Rob Hall decided to break his own rules that were communicated clearly to the entire team and attempt the summit after 2 pm. We will never know if it was because he was cognitively compromised or if he just really wanted one of his clients to summit, as he, his client and another expedition leader died on the mountain when an unexpected storm came in.

Where is the client in the hierarchy?

There is an added complexity in expedition teams which also arises in corporate consultancies. The client certainly needs to be part of the team, however when we have a master–servant relationship with the client it becomes difficult for the experts to provide guidance in the way that they see fit. When the client is so prescriptive – *I am paying you to get me to the top of the mountain no matter what* – it makes it difficult for the Sherpa to say it's unsafe and you can always try again next year.

This arises also in engineering or construction projects when the client dictates so much of the project without listening to the reasons why a certain approach was selected. The consultancy is bullied into doing the project in a way that they do not recommend, and this turns into a blame game very quickly if there is a problem. Establishing early in the relationship the parameters of the client/service provider agreement is important to avoid costly problems and miscommunication.

STAYING TRUE TO YOURSELF

When we spend enough time in an outcome-focused role we will eventually come to a situation where we are faced with a quandary: *should we do what is right or what will deliver results?* My Sherpa was very clear on what he had to deliver to his client. He said to me: 'it is my job to get you safely to Base Camp, that is what you have paid me for'. We were trekking with other people, and although he would assist them he knew his only goal was to get me there. The values of safety and customer service were very high in his work. A saying he used a lot on that trek and still uses today is 'you happy, me happy'. He was keen on delivering a superior experience to his clients and he knew he had achieved that when the client was smiling. When his client smiled, they were also more likely to recommend him to others and give him a good tip.

This was all well and good until he had a cranky customer and no matter what he did they were not going to be happy. After the 2015 earthquake he was leading a German couple who wanted to continue walking up the mountain even though everyone else was coming down and they were going to do it with or without him. He stayed with them because it was his job to try to keep them safe, but because he knew they would be safest if they started to descend this action went against his values. It was difficult for him to decide what to do. Fortunately after the trekkers witnessed the number of people who were descending and they talked to a group of Germans who explained what was happening, the reluctantly agreed to descend with Gobinda (much to my relief when I spoke to him on the phone).

My Sherpa was blessed to have discovered what his role and his values were – they were simple but they were clear. But not everyone is as clear in what their values are and why they should keep alignment. Working for a long time in a role that is not aligned with your values will likely lead to burnout regardless of the size of the paycheque, and this applies to your team members as well. When personal and work values are not aligned the result is employee dissatisfaction and business failure. It also becomes important to recognise when those around you are wrangling with some dissonance, to try to help them achieve alignment or at least recognise what is happening.

A simple brain dump of what motivates you, what makes you smile and what part of your job gives you satisfaction will serve you well. If spending time with family is high on your values and you are doing a role that keeps you away from them, that is not alignment. If you are working for a mining company and are a staunch environmentalist this is also difficult to reckon with. However, it may be less obvious: working for a leader who is reactive when you like to have time to organise your day can also contribute to dissonance.

What are my values?	What brings me joy?	What frustrates me?
Honesty	Delivery of projects	Clients who do not take the time to fully understand a project
Accountability	A fun team	Working with people who I do not respect
Peace	Problem solving	Justifying my reasoning to someone who has no understanding of the problem

Above are some thoughts to prompt your thinking; grab a pen and consider your truth. What are your values? What brings you joy and what frustrates you? Write it down – obtaining this clarity is an excellent first step. Live and work according to your values to stay aligned and reduce the stress in your life.

Lessons from a Sherpa

- Speak up if there is something wrong – there is no such thing as a stupid question. Your perspective is different and you may be able to see something others can't. Together you can work on a solution to the problem you have identified.
- Appreciate your team and value their contribution. Understand and take advantage of the different personalities in your group.
- A Sherpa is a trekking guide, porter, translator, waiter, builder, counsellor, tea maker, cleaner, parent, offspring and many more. A title does not define them. They will do what is required at the time it is required and work with a wide variety of people to make the experience the best possible. All they ask is that you appreciate them as a whole person and not just a trekking guide.
- Their job is to get you up and back safely, not to get you to the top no matter what. They are there to support you and provide a safe journey.
- We all make mistakes. We need to have an environment where it is acceptable to make a mistake and learn from it. If we feel like we need to hide a mistake more will inevitably follow.

EIGHT

SUPPORT

*'Anyone can support a team that is winning – it takes
no courage. But to defend a team when it is down and
really needs you, that takes a lot of courage.'*

Bart Starr, former American football coach

Supporting each other in a team is vital. Knowing that someone else has your back is essential to be able do your job and know that when you need it you will have help.

I would like to introduce a bridge as a metaphor for a supportive team: the pillars of the bridge need to support the weight of the road over a large span to allow the traffic to flow above it. Not a lot of thought is given to the pillars and the vital role they play in allowing everything to continue as designed. But if you didn't have the supporting pillars, or if you didn't have enough of them or if a couple of them were not structurally sound, the bridge would fall down, cars would fall off and people would be severely injured; in short, it would be a disaster.

We need a lot of support and the right support to keep the bridge upright – but it is more than that. Shawn Achor's research into happiness showed that 'social support is the greatest predictor of happiness during periods of high stress'. In addition to this though, Shawn also found that people who provide social support to others at work were 10 times more likely to be engaged and 40% more likely to get a promotion!

It turns out that when we invest in supporting others, we also feel good and reap the returns. When we show support to our team our connection improves, we feel appreciated and thus are more engaged. When you have a team who look out for each other and offer each other support it is a sign of genuine care and consideration. This support should ideally come from all members of the team, not just the leader; we have just seen that we need many pillars to hold up the bridge. The responsibility of the leader is to instil a culture where supporting our colleagues is the norm – this will be advantageous to all.

There are many aspects to supporting others in the team, which fall into three key areas:

- ▲ showing compassion
- ▲ lending a hand
- ▲ setting new starters up for success.

We have looked at these three aspects throughout the book.

When they are on the mountain, Sherpas know they can call on each other when needed. There is no hierarchy or worrying about who does what. They just do what needs to be done. On the mountain, your life can depend on your teammates having your back when you need it, and being able to trust each other to do the work properly.

THE SILENT KILLER

In recent times there has been a significant increase in mental illness, instances of suicide and a general reduction in mental health and wellbeing in the Western world. The statistics have long shown that one in five people are working with a mental illness. This means that a member of your team is likely to be suffering with a mental illness at any given time.

They call it the silent killer because often people do not talk about how they are feeling and do not want to voice their concerns. Whether we admit it or not there is still a stigma attached to having a mental illness, although that is shifting. We have all heard a story of someone who seemed to be fine, they never said anything was wrong, they looked to 'have it all together', but who was suffering from depression or tragically took their own life.

When researching for this book I came across a statistic: 38% of people surveyed by Sane Research had not disclosed their mental illness to their employer. Although disclosing a mental illness is a personal choice, I found this to be a worrying statistic as the respondents also stated that they felt there was a stigma associated with mental illness. The research was conducted in 2011 so I disregarded the statistic, believing that our workplaces have become better at normalising mental health struggles. So imagine my surprise when I reviewed the Wellbeing Lab Workplace Report 2020; the data was collected through COVID-19 and it conveyed that only 16.6% of Australians feel safe sharing their struggles at work and mental health is the leading cause of their struggles.

This statistic is confronting, and it reaffirms that our colleagues need our support. Reflecting on the bridge analogy, it is very clear that we need as many pillars as possible to support the team. Although not a silver bullet to relieve mental illness, embracing a truly flexible approach to work will certainly assist us in managing our competing priorities.

Most workplace experts agree the increase in workplace flexibility is a positive change, however we need to be conscious that it's more difficult to support a team when they are geographically dispersed. Many of us are in the process of re-evaluating our priorities and are more aware of the team's different motivators, desires and values. We know that the workload can change, personal issues can arise and commitments can alter quite unexpectedly. An illness or death in a family will change priorities in an instant. When we have the support of the pillars to hold us, we can overcome whatever setbacks come our way. It may be that the pillars need to be stronger or need to listen a little closer when we are working remotely. Being mindful that most people are not comfortable reaching out and letting employers or co-workers know when they are struggling is important and should influence your approach.

We do not need to understand the details of the mental illness, and it is unlikely you will fully understand unless you have experienced it. When we remember, 'You never really understand a person until you consider things from his point of view, until you climb into his skin and walk around in it,' as Harper Lee wrote in *To Kill a Mockingbird*, we can start the journey to genuine compassion.

FASHIONABLE COMPASSION

When my Sherpa and I had to say goodbye to our beautiful Labrador x Doberman, Montana, our vet Dr Anthony was with us every step of the way. We met five years previously when he had a conversation with us about my 10-year-old rottweiler Dakota (Gobinda had only been in Australia three months at this point). She had bone cancer and likely only had weeks to live. When we said our goodbyes to Dakota, my Sherpa had no understanding of why I was so sad that my dog was dying. Dr Anthony was compassionate and kind yet direct in his communication. I was left with no question about what he was trying to tell me as he spoke in a clear, easy communication style, yet still had the ability to show compassion. Direct communicators can be regarded as lacking compassion, but Dr Anthony is a master at both. It is a skill you can learn. It is a valuable skill and it is at the heart of being able to have an effective 'courageous conversation'.

Dr Anthony delivers exceedingly difficult information to pet owners every day of the week. However, when you meet him, you feel that the only thing he has to do for that day is talk to you. He is fully present, maintains eye contact and has a knowing look that conveys a deep understanding of what you are feeling. The work that Dr Anthony does is immensely emotionally draining, yet he doesn't try to take the easy way out and just treat you like a number – he makes sure you know that he cares for the whole family. He must have to dig down into the depths of his own emotions to give that to his clients, but he is so passionate about giving animals the best end to their life he couldn't think about doing it any other way. 'Happy life, happy death' is his mantra and we should all be so lucky. When it came time to say our final goodbyes to Montana I was giving her some treats, but this was not good enough for my Sherpa. He went to the fridge and brought down a full rump steak that she enjoyed as her final meal. It was the most loving act I had seen him show towards our dogs and it caused me to break down in tears for a raft of reasons.

The experience of saying goodbye to the soul that had been with us through our relationship was very difficult for us both and it got me thinking about compassion, empathy and sympathy. We often use the terms interchangeably, however understanding the difference makes it easier for those who are driven more by intellect than emotion to implement compassion into communication and leadership.

Yogic and Buddhist tradition teaches us that empathy is viscerally feeling what another feels. Research into mirror neurons has shown that empathy may arise automatically when you witness someone in pain. For example, if you saw me slam a car door on my fingers, you might feel pain in your fingers as well.

Sympathy on the other hand is when you can imagine or understand how someone else is feeling, but you do not actually feel it. When we are compassionate, we go a step further; not only do you feel the pain of another (empathy) or you recognise that the person is in pain (sympathy), you also do your best to alleviate the person's suffering from that situation.

At its Latin roots 'compassion' means 'to suffer with'. When you are compassionate, you are not avoiding suffering, you're not feeling overwhelmed by it and you're not pretending the suffering doesn't exist. When you practise compassion, you can stay present with suffering. Showing compassion can help you gain a new point of view because it puts you in someone else's shoes and allows you to focus on alleviating someone's suffering.

Dr Anthony knows that when he ends a pet's suffering, he will enhance the owner's suffering but he also knows that in time, the knowledge that they gave their pet a 'happy death' will offer comfort. Dr Anthony treats the whole family with compassion. He doesn't sugar coat it. He knows that there is pain, but he ensures that owners are equipped to make the best decision at the right time.

As leaders we can learn from this approach. Delivering unpleasant information in a clear and compassionate style so it is well received and tapping into our emotions that may be uncomfortable shows authenticity and results in respect.

A team that can show compassion to one another will support each other when required, because they have developed an understanding of how their teammate is feeling and they want to make it easier for them.

GRAPPLING WITH PETER PERFECT

Have you ever worked with someone who will never admit a mistake? It is bamboozling to me why they would spend the energy arguing that the sky is green when they have clearly just made a mistake. The most pragmatic approach is to admit the mistake, apologise and present a solution; after all, what recourse can be administered against you when you have determined a solution?

I have spent time pondering why not everyone sees it that way. The reason generally boils down to a phenomenon called 'cognitive dissonance'; when you know what it is and recognise when you or those around you may be experiencing it, it becomes invaluable in navigating workplace interactions and working more effectively in a team. Cognitive dissonance is a mental discomfort that results from holding two conflicting beliefs, values or attitudes. When there is inconsistency between what people believe and how they behave this causes them to seek to minimise the discomfort by acting in a way that reduces the inconsistency. For example: Danny believes he is an excellent team member, but he got very frustrated by a member of his team and sent a rude email to his colleague and cc'd their manager. It is clear for all to see that Danny made a mistake by sending the email in anger, but because he strongly believes he is a good team member and his actions had been so contrary to that belief he has two choices. He can either:

- look at the evidence, admit he made a mistake, apologise and find a way to repair the relationship and navigate to a solution
- try to justify his actions by blaming the colleague because he 'drove him to it' by being incompetent or blaming the boss because he is not managing the colleague well.

Carol Tavris, co-author of the book *Mistakes Were Made (But Not by Me)*, points out that cognitive dissonance threatens our sense of self. 'To reduce dissonance, we have to modify the self-concept or accept the evidence,' Tavris said. The other option (generally the one taken), of course, is to justify your mistake.

Cognitive dissonance is uncomfortable, and everyone experiences it to some degree. To recognise it, there are some signs that you can look for:

- feeling uncomfortable before deciding or taking action
- trying to justify or rationalise a decision or action you have made

- feeling embarrassed about something you have done and trying to hide your actions from other people
- experiencing guilt or regret about something you have done in the past.

I have known many managers who have considered it a weakness to admit a mistake. When coaching them through this thought process it eventually becomes apparent to them that to lead authentically you need to be honest and acknowledge that you are not perfect. What you ultimately must overcome is the cognitive dissonance you are experiencing.

Another example of when you may experience cognitive dissonance is if you believe yourself to be a reliable and organised person and you forget to do something. You are faced with the choice:

a) admit it and fix it
b) justify why it was missed.

In nearly every case option 'a' is the easiest, quickest and best solution, however it requires you to admit you made a mistake and wrangle with the cognitive dissonance that presents. When it's obvious that a mistake was made, digging your heels in demonstrates your weakness of character rather than strength. Self-reflect, show vulnerability, admit your mistake and strive to improve. This will result in respect from your team.

On the mountain, mistakes are easily discoverable and attempting to cover them up will result in a dangerous situation. My Sherpa and those I have met are humble and would not enter into the ego-driven behaviour of thinking that they are infallible. They are honest and will do what is right. *I made a mistake, I am sorry – can you please help me fix it?* It is how problems are solved and how they learn, then as they get better they can then support the new members of a Sherpa team.

BUILDING ANTIFRAGILITY

In this decade of disruption, it is important that we have people in our teams who can thrive during uncertainty. Dr Paige Williams in her book *Becoming Antifragile* proposes the skill we need to build in individuals, teams and organisations is antifragility. She simplifies the concept by concluding that the essence of becoming antifragile is being prepared for what we can't predict. This to me seems like the key skill for now and into the future.

Author Brooke Castillo of the Life Coach School Podcast explores the difference between being fragile, robust and antifragile. She explains when we are robust or resilient, we can encounter adversity and have the inner fortitude to overcome it. To be antifragile, we sit in the feeling, experience it and analyse how and why we reacted how we did. This practice enables us to not just overcome the situation but learn how we felt, why we felt this way and develop techniques that will help us when we encounter adversity in the future. When we are antifragile, each challenging experience results in us being less fragile in the future – not more, as is the case when adversity chips away at our resilience one setback at a time.

Research by Beyond Blue suggests that one-quarter of Australians will experience an anxiety condition in their lifetime, and that one in six has experienced anxiety or depression in the last 12 months. Building our antifragility is one way of combating anxiety. Anxiety is effectively fear of the unknown, and when we are antifragile we believe we can deal with the unknown because we have taken the time to work through the process before.

The challenge for an organisation is to hold the space for employees so they feel comfortable to experience a troubling emotion and learn from it. When there is an issue encountered in the workplace the first reaction is to fix it. Once it is rectified a 'lessons learnt' approach may be instigated. This has the potential to become a litany of excuses. If we sit longer with the problem and work through the impact on the organisation and how to create an environment where the organisation is not exposed to risk, the outcome is more positive. The team is learning how to bounce back together, not how to protect the individual.

Effectively, when we allow people to make mistakes and learn from them, we are building antifragility. When we have an environment where we hide small mistakes until they combine into a catastrophic one, and the people involved do not know how to cope with making mistakes, we are setting the organisation up for disaster. As a leader you can assist in this process by normalising small mistakes, giving an anecdote of when you have done a similar thing and talk through how it made you feel, how it was rectified and what you learnt. A bit of humour does not go astray, and it encourages the admitting of mistakes in the future to all of those in the team. The more opportunities we have to build antifragility with mistakes that can be readily rectified the better off the organisation is.

EMBRACE QUESTIONING FOR IMPROVEMENT

Questioning is how we learn; the toddler in the 'but why' phase shows us that the curiosity is there and they truly want to understand more about their surroundings and their role in them. This does not detract from the fact that it is very annoying. When we have team members who are regularly questioning at work, this can be perceived similarly. The leaders of old would have said something akin to, 'Just do your damn job'. We may be tempted to think they do not trust the leadership or the decisions being made. Some leaders may go as far as suspecting they are using questioning as a delaying tactic so they do not have to muck in and get the job done. Another perspective may be that they are resistant to change. However, giving people the benefit of the doubt, it could be that they just seek to understand the reasons things are the way they are to see if things can be done better.

When an organisation is looking to embed a continuous improvement culture it is important that there are people who are questioning the decisions and thinking of ways it can be done better. It is our challenge as leaders to not take this as a threat or think that the feedback is designed to show we are wrong. If we do find questioning behaviour threatening, it may be time to do a bit of soul searching to find out why that may be and how we can learn to respect the opinions of others.

It takes courage to question the status quo and we need to have these people in the organisation to challenge us. We should not expect our team to follow us blindly like sheep, for it is when we are uncomfortable that we all truly grow. Allowing your employees to question and listen fully before making judgement is a sign of respect; it shows humility and reinforces that you really are interested in improving things in your team.

It is important that we show respect for employees as it has been found that the most important thing leaders should demonstrate is respect. It ranked above recognition, communicating an inspiring vision, providing feedback and even opportunities for growth. In a study conducted by *Harvard Business Review* and Tony Schwartz, those who get respect from their leaders reported 56% better health and wellbeing, 72% more trust and safety, 89% greater enjoyment and satisfaction with their jobs and 92% greater focus and prioritisation than those who didn't.

Respect also has a clear impact on engagement. The more leaders give, the higher the level of employee engagement: people who said leaders treated them with respect were 55% more engaged. No one respects a sheep; they may be liked for allowing the leader to walk the easy path but those who question appropriately and are invested in improvement are the employees who will propel us to the next level and deserve our respect. The leaders who learn to show respect to their team will have better engagement and productivity and their team will ultimately make their life easier.

SUPPORT TO BE THEIR BEST

The way employees deliver a service is directly proportional to how they feel about the company. To expect an employee to treat customers differently to how they are treated by the company is insanity. The principles that govern how you run the company should be congruent with company aspirations, and indeed congruent with an employee's individual values to encourage employees to feel committed to the organisation and deliver on the vision.

A company principle might be 'we value our people', however if they are not able to employ more people when the workload increases and so employees receive a hit to the work–life balance, that principle is not in line with the aspiration to be an employer of choice. Alternately, a principle may be a dedication to safety but if the personal protective equipment cupboard is bare they are not living to this value.

Stephen R Covey wrote:

If you take care of your employees, they will take care of your business and your business will take care of itself.

I think it's helpful to take that further; decide the vision of the company, determine the principles needed to get there, support employees to deliver services in line with those principles, then your aspiration will be realised and the company will propel forward.

THE TRAINING INVESTMENT

There is a cost in achieving a company vision, and in most cases this is investing in your employees, be that their learning, development and professional improvement or simply offering the support required for them to get on with their jobs. This does not have to be in the form of traditional training, it can be – and this is usually more effective – in the form of workshops, coaching or mentoring, where employees have the ability to contribute and feel valued.

Likewise, when aspiring to be an employer of choice in your industry, there will be a price to pay. It may be investing in training your staff, it may be offering development opportunities, it may be ensuring your leaders have the support required to spend time on employee engagement. Regardless of the price, it will be worth it because when you are investing in employee engagement the returns are limitless.

Sadly, the training and development budget is often the first to go when an organisation is required to cut costs – this makes little sense to me. When the economy takes a dive, if you want to get ahead of the competition, it is an ideal time to invest in the people you have in the organisation. They are the ones who are going to be relied upon to lead the company out of the downturn.

Richard Branson's famous line puts it perfectly, and it is so obvious – so why do many companies still have this attitude?

> *Train your employees so they can leave. Treat them well enough so they don't want to.*

When we have a long-term approach to developing our people, we garner their investment in the organisation. This needs to start from the moment that they join. Nearly every manager wants their employees to 'hit the ground running', but I believe this expectation of a new employee is unfair and not setting them up for success.

Hiring employees with the required skills and experience to bring to the role is entirely different to expecting employees to hit the ground running and produce the best they are capable of without an appropriate level of support. The problem with employing somebody to hit the ground running is that you are seeking a robot to achieve a required outcome. Robots will do what you tell them to, the way that they have been programmed, but they will do no more. They don't think outside the box, they don't create innovative solutions, there's no questioning, there's no thought about continuous improvement.

Therefore, expecting employees to hit the ground running is to your detriment.

When Gobinda first arrived from Nepal to live with me, we encountered a few teething problems. When we spent our first 30 days together in Nepal, we were not doing any cooking or cleaning as we were travelling and buying all our meals. His trip to Australia was the first time he had left Nepal. One day I asked him to clean the dishes and left him to it. When I came back, there was water flying all over the kitchen. I exasperatedly raised my voice and asked him what he thought he was doing. He smiled at me without turning off the tap and said, 'I am cleaning dish'. What my Sherpa had done was stack all the dishes in the sink, turned on the tap, and he was using his hand to swipe away any food remnants along with the streaming water to clean the dishes. In his method there was no need for a dishcloth or washing liquid let alone a plug. 'That's not how you do it,' I told him. He looked at me genuinely confused as this was clearly the only way he had ever been taught to clean dishes. It struck me at that moment that my way was not the 'right way', it was just the 'Australian way'. I took the time to show him the purpose of the plug, washing liquid, cloth, dish rack, and how to reduce the force of the water through the flick mixer. Fortunately, with this guidance, he has been adequately (I believe in picking your battles) washing the household dishes ever since.

The way that we are first taught something is the way we believe to be 'right' until we are convinced that there may be an alternative approach. When someone new starts in a job there is a time of acculturation where they are learning about the ways the new culture approaches tasks. This can often be make or break, particularly when an employee is early in their career or has had a significant change in circumstances leading up to this role. If the employee is lacking in self-confidence they may not stand up and explain why they are doing something a certain way, and often more training is required with some employees.

According to *Training Industry Quarterly* it takes between 12 and 24 months to become fully productive in a new role, and that is dependent on the degree of training put in during the first six months. It's the role of the manager and team to set the new starter up for success by investing in training and projecting a feeling of approachability. The new starter needs to feel able to ask questions and put forward ideas and their point of view to have a fair probation period.

I have lost count of the number of times I have been asked by a manager to terminate an employee during the probation period because it seemed like the easiest option. They clearly were not able to spend quality time up front with the employee, which should be the highest priority for them. I always question: are they doing a task wrong, or just differently? Have you taken the time to talk through the way you would like it done? Are they willing to improve and enthusiastic about learning? This paints a picture of whether it was a wrong hire, or they need more support to be successful. I am not against terminating in probation and sometimes it can be the best outcome, however asking if something is wrong or simply different can help clarify what is really going on.

It amuses me when managers think all their problems will be solved at the point of hire. No recruitment process is flawless. We are dealing with flawed humans to begin with, and far too often I have seen the 'hit the ground running' paradigm fall short. If you cannot invest in the new starter, you cannot afford the new starter. If you have little to invest, their return will be the limited to the return of a substandard employee.

The commonly held belief is that the investment required is an oppressive amount of time to be carved out of your tight schedule. However, the truth is that if you have the right systems, level of organisation and energy to invest the actual time will be minimal and the returns maximal. One in five millennials do not pass their probation period, and employees whose companies have longer onboarding programs gain full proficiency 34% more quickly than those in the shortest programs.

Case study: The wrong way or a different way?

Ramsha had recently arrived from Iran when she gained a position in project controls in an Australian engineering firm. She was left to her own devices to do the job for the first couple of weeks as she had experience in a similar role in her home country. Her manager realised that she was not producing work to the level that he expected, and he went to complain to Human Resources. They asked how much support Ramsha was being given and details of what was not satisfactory in her work. It became clear that the likely reason the work was substandard was because she had not been informed of the manager's and client's expectations.

The manager allocated different members of the team to sit with her and show her areas for improvement, and she was shadowed for a few weeks – her work improved. Ramsha was relieved to be getting more detailed guidance as she was very unsure about working in Australia as the company worked quite differently to what she was used to. She also appreciated having better interactions with the team as she did not feel confident speaking up in a group setting because everyone else knew each other and she really felt like an outsider. Getting the one-on-one guidance improved her confidence and she started to feel like she was contributing better to the organisation. The level of engagement in her work improved. She had been considering leaving the organisation and was questioning if she could make the transition to Australian work life.

Mantra:

GO WITH THE FLOW

Providing support gives people the confidence
to ask questions and feel psychologically
safe in the environment.

We can act like a Sherpa by supporting, guiding, introducing and giving advice to the new starter. Working together like a mountaineering team, the new starter can be supported to reach the summit in the safest, most efficient way with a focus on developing into the role.

It is all about synchronicity. Synchronising the new starter with the expectations of them. Synchronising them with the team. Synchronising their skills with the role. Synchronising their efforts with what experience shows the areas of focus should be. When a mountaineering team invests in the first three months when they bring on a new Sherpa they are providing support to set everyone up for success. At the end of the three months (in a Sherpa's world, it is likely less) they know with clarity if it has been the right hire and can make a confident decision at the end of the first summit season. You can decide if the new starter can now hit the ground running armed with all they have learned in the first three months.

Not all new starters are successful in their roles, but this should not be looked upon as failure. It was a successful process because it provided further clarity on the process, the role and the person you need to fill it.

Lessons from a Sherpa

- You can never truly understand how another person is feeling, but you can step inside their boots and spend time thinking about how you would feel in them. Once you have gained this understanding it makes it possible to better support them.
- If someone makes a mistake, help them fix it; this is how they learn.
- If you need help, ask. This is how you learn to trust and connect with others.
- When we support each other we all reap the rewards.
- People do not know what is expected of them unless they are told. Make expectations clear so they can be met or exceeded.

NINE

DIRECTION

'The biggest concern for any organization should be when their most passionate people become quiet.'

Tim McClure, professional speaker and leadership consultant

Providing direction is a key aspect of leadership. Getting the team on the trail and aligned to where they need to go is essential. If you have ever used the term 'herding cats', you will understand that getting everyone aligned on the path forward makes achieving any team goal considerably easier. But providing direction in a Sherpa's world is also leading by example, in line with your values, being flexible and listening to those around you. One thing that I know for sure is that you can't hurry a Sherpa; they are contemplative souls who will arrive at the destination when they get there. The tourists are constantly asking, 'how far is it?', 'when will we get there?' and 'what time will we arrive?', and the Sherpa responds with 'a little bit up and a little bit down' and a vague gesticulation in the direction of the destination. They know that the trail leads to the destination, and if something changes the route they will look at the situation when they need to and evaluate the next best way forward. The main thing is that they keep moving as the best Sherpa they can be, not that they know when they will arrive.

LEAD WITH INTEGRITY

Being a leader so you can look in the mirror and be happy with what you see is essential to a sustainable career. Difficult decisions will need to be made and difficult messages delivered, but if they are conveyed with honesty and fairness it will result in respect from your team, not disillusionment. Treat people fairly and work to gain trust through authenticity. There are personalities that we would prefer to work with and employees who we resonate with more, but look objectively at the decisions you make and the way you deliver a message. Would it pass the 'front page of the newspaper test'? Do some work to become aware of your unconscious biases, and ask for input from those in your team for areas you could improve, and then actively work to improve.

A leader with integrity is able to convey the vision and assist the team to achieve the work required to make that vision a reality. If you can motivate your team in a meaningful way and be true to yourself, your team and your values, you will come across as an authentic leader who can be relied upon.

According to research by futurist Jacob Morgan released in 2019, 1200 CEOs around the globe identified the most important skills for leaders as being able to:

- ▲ motivate, engage and inspire employees
- ▲ listen to and communicate with their workforce

- look at different scenarios and possibilities
- display emotional intelligence.

But a LinkedIn survey showed 63% of respondents described their CEOs as doing 'somewhat well' or 'not well at all' on key leadership qualities, with Australian leaders coming out the worst out of the 12 countries surveyed.

The fact that executives believed they were doing well in the key areas yet the employees strongly disagreed led Morgan to conclude that the executives were too removed from the business. This highlights the importance of staying in contact with the day to day and the issues that employees are facing.

To lead with integrity is to utterly understand the concerns of your workforce and not just pay lip service. A good team will see through that quickly and lose respect. Show that you care, have given due consideration to the issues and believe that you can work with the team to improve the situation and you will earn a reputation as an authentic leader that people are driven to follow.

Case study: A distrustful culture

A large resources company was driving a culture change and they were getting the managers to ask for feedback from their people about areas they and the company could improve on. The employees were assured the feedback would be taken on board and that they should feel safe to share what they thought of the culture, leadership and the way that the business was being run.

Those in the organisation who were trusting and believed that they should share information to improve things unfortunately did so at their employment peril. There were people whose contracts were not renewed, or they were bullied by their managers until they quit, and in one extreme case were tricked into breaking the code of conduct and subsequently sacked.

Those who were left in the organisation learnt that speaking truthfully and calling out bad behaviour is punished with a very difficult existence in that company. Unsurprisingly employees stopped speaking up and they just went about their roles, not caring to improve things. What resulted was a distrustful culture and employees went into cover-your-arse mode; they did not support each other and a group of 'dobbers' was born.

If you are going to ask for feedback ensure that you are prepared to hear and act on what is said. Unless this is the case, the feedback will stop or it will become feedback fuelled by lies because that is what the manager clearly wants to hear.

Mantra:

GO WITH THE FLOW

In the 'obliged' culture, doing the bare minimum
and not caring about the business is
the easiest way to survive.

DO WHAT IS RIGHT

The role that our values play in our lives cannot be under-stated. Reflecting upon past momentous decisions that you have made in your life, I propose that the reason you made each decision was to move your life closer to your values or to ensure your integrity was not violated by having to do something in contradiction to your values. When we live a life congruent with our values we have a contented existence.

When you have faith in your ability to make a difference it is amazing where the support comes from. Don't be afraid to back yourself. If you see something that you know in your heart is not right it is your duty, firstly, to those who are affected but also to yourself to act.

There may be times when you are not the person who is standing up against an injustice; in these times, recognise that being the person who supports others is just as valuable. Whether you take a stand or support someone taking a stand you are ensuring that the culture you want to work in is maintained or has the chance to be attained. When you or your team is asked to do something that is contrary to the values of the team, banding together and uniting to have your voices heard can improve the culture. If on the other hand no one chooses to stand up, this can – in the long run – break the fibre that is holding the culture together.

Often it is hard to stand up for what is right; trust me, I have done it and have the mental scars to prove it, but at times you have little choice. I have stood up to a narcissistic bully in the workplace and called out their behaviour to my personal and professional detriment. People supported me through that time, and I will be eternally grateful for that – never underestimate the importance of support. In the end, not only did my actions call out the toxic culture that had been considered acceptable, it gave other employees the courage to stand up for themselves and remove themselves from the situation.

This experience taught me that when you live according to your values, are kind, show respect, take a stand for the collective and support those who need some extra strength, not only will success follow, so will fulfillment in your life.

ANTICIPATE SETBACKS

On the mountain, the ability to anticipate problems is essential to success. Be one step ahead of the setbacks and stay in a proactive space rather than falling into firefighter mode. As we examined earlier in the book, anticipation trumps reaction.

There is a difference however between anticipating problems and dwelling on them. Anticipating and planning to overcome setbacks is a positive way to deal with the inevitable issues that arise. A practical way to anticipate potential setbacks is to encourage others to identify and anticipate problems and share their thoughts. However, this should not be perceived as accepting complaining in the team. When we allow complaining to infiltrate a team the positive and collaborative culture can quickly evaporate.

When leading a team, it's important to actively listen. When we are provided with ideas, feedback and information, if we consider the suggestions fully it is easier for us to achieve team goals. Even if the solutions presented are not able to be implemented, it is advisable to talk through the reasons why not to improve team engagement. When we ask for feedback we will, of course, encounter people who are just passionate about whinging. In those cases, you may need to redirect that passion to focus on a positive outlook. Help them to focus on finding a solution rather than whinging about the problem. When you redirect their focus, the passion and energy can be leveraged for improvement.

In addition to anticipating setbacks, instil a practice of anticipating successes to provide motivation. Empowering the team to anticipate and feel the elation of the expected success will serve as inspiration to keep moving towards the goal. The team will feel like winners before they have achieved the goal and that is a powerful driver to keep going.

Anticipation is one of the most integral aspects of a successful team – this is especially true if the team are geographically dispersed. Anticipate setbacks to remain in a proactive space and anticipate successes to keep the energy of the team high so they sail through the setbacks. A remote team made up of winners takes the time to anticipate problems and plan how they will overcome them. They recognise that making plans for potential setbacks is smart but dwelling on them is not. They do not tolerate whingers. Winners love operating in the positive environment gained by anticipating success. Winners see the successful possibilities that whingers cannot visualise because their minds are filled with all the reasons why they cannot succeed. On the mountain this means always having confidence that you will get to your next milestone on the trek, and if you keep doing that you will eventually reach the summit. Sherpas know that a negative mindset can undermine a whole team and therefore a whole expedition.

DO WHAT YOU SAY YOU WILL

At the essence of creating trust in any relationship is this simple responsibility: do what you say you are going to do. If you cannot deliver on a piece of work or meet a deadline let the recipient know why. Call it out early and clearly and work to deliver the next best outcome. When you build a reputation as someone who does what they say they are going to do, you will earn the trust and respect of those around you. If you are authentic this will translate into transparency, open communication, and in turn engagement with those around you.

One of my favourite stories my Dad tells is from when he was 19. He'd recently arrived in Brisbane from country Victoria and was playing football at the local Australian Rules football club. He learnt that one of his mates had got himself into a spot of bother and was being held at the Surfers Paradise watch house and needed to be bailed out. My Dad did not have any money (and neither did any of his friends), so he summoned the courage to ask one of the patrons of the club for a loan (I believe it was the equivalent of a week's wages at the time). He gave Dad the money (good on him) and Dad bailed out his mate, and a month or so later Dad went back to the patron when he was celebrating a win at the bar and returned the loan. Apparently he was in shock. He laughed, and said he never expected to see that money again, and he bought Dad a beer.

Anyone who knows my Dad knows that there was never any doubt he was going to give the money back – it was only a matter of when he could get the funds together. He accumulated the money without contribution from the felon mate; it was Dad's responsibility. He said he would give it back, so he did. In that instance, he overdelivered to the expectations that the patron had, and you can bet my Dad had his trust for life.

Where there is trust, there is a reduction in micromanagement, greater motivation to exceed expectations, and teams work together to help each other for the greater good. If you are confident that your teammates will deliver you don't waste energy wondering what they are up to and you focus on delivering your own work. Creating a culture of trust is an important aspect of leadership and is priceless for engagement and productivity. Do what you say you are going to do; underpromise and overdeliver. It is a lot easier to direct a team to the summit when they are surrounded by people they trust. They will more easily accept help and consider an alternate route if it comes from people they trust.

BEHAVIOUR IS LEARNED – LEARNING IS LIFELONG

If it's decided that the direction of the organisation needs to shift it is likely prompted by a shift in beliefs. For some reason, someone, somewhere decided that the culture was not what is required and a change must be made. A change in the beliefs is needed to prompt a change in behaviour, and for the beliefs to change there must be some motivation to do so.

For example: if I stop believing that my boss has it in for me and start being a bit more open to their feedback my day-to-day interactions with them might improve:

1   *Motivation:* A better work environment and reducing my anxiety.
2   *Belief:* Change from 'my boss is trying to sack me' to 'he is giving me an opportunity to grow by highlighting areas for improvement'.
3   *Behaviour:* Once the new belief takes hold my behaviour shifts to focusing on my improvement, not fearing my boss.

1   *Motivation:* I would like more support from my colleagues.
2   *Belief:* Change from 'they take me for granted' to 'they don't know how to show appreciation'.
3   *Behaviour:* Once the new belief takes hold you start modelling appreciation and it is contagious.

The culture of an organisation is unlikely to change unless there is a focus on the behaviour that is accepted and the beliefs that drive the behaviour. We learn how to behave from those around us. Sherpas know that demonstrating expected team behaviours is much more powerful than telling people what to do. A child will follow its family's behaviour to understand what is acceptable. Some families are very affectionate, and the child will learn to hug and kiss; other children will grow up thinking that a pat on the back is the height of affection. There is nothing wrong with either of the behaviours within that family culture, but when the child starts interacting with other families they may change their behaviour in different situations.

The same is true for work teams. Over time, a certain set of behaviours becomes acceptable and entrenched in the culture. These behaviours may contribute to improving the culture, such as giving support and appreciation to each other. They can also be detrimental to the culture, such as gossiping or whinging about a problem with no intention to try to improve things.

You may be aware of the above the line and below the line model – this is referenced in Carolyn Taylor's book *Walking the Talk: Building a culture for success*. She is an organisational culture expert and states that she was introduced to the concept by Robert Kiyosaki (author of *Rich Dad Poor Dad*). I often think of the model in terms of the great John McClane line in the movie *Die Hard*: 'If you are not part of the solution, you are part of the problem'. I believe that the way you behave every day in your team determines if you are above the line (part of the solution) or below the line (part of the problem). Once the effort is put in to change some detrimental behaviours, the cumulative effect for other behaviours is like a rock rolling down a hill – it gathers momentum and the team are collectively striving to be the best they can be.

Often it might only require a slight change in perspective towards the belief or motivation to change the behaviour and in turn the culture. To direct yourself and your team towards the behaviours that will benefit you and your team, a simple above the line/below the line analysis may be all it takes. The direction the team culture is taking is a sum of individual behaviours in the team. All behaviour is learned, and if there are only a few people directing the behaviour it can be picked up by all.

To be an effective leader of others you need to first lead yourself and know the direction you are heading. To be your best self and model the behaviour you want to see from others you need to know what your best self looks like. Who are you striving to become? This means developing personal goals and checking in on them regularly. These may be smart goals that are written in a diary or more detailed goals covering all aspects of your life that you are working towards. When people around you see that you are taking your personal development seriously, they start to do the same. The real journey we are all on is to become the best versions of ourselves. Imagine a world where everyone is on this journey of getting one step better every day. Most people who set out to climb Everest are on that journey but some are not; they are always the worst team members who no one wants to support or spend much time with. To be a leader you must work out where you are going individually as a person and work out who you need to become to get there.

Lessons from a Sherpa

- ▲ Always know where you are and where you are going.
- ▲ Where you are is not good or bad, it just is; you need to work out a plan to get to where you want to be.
- ▲ People follow those they trust – put your effort into being a trustworthy leader.
- ▲ You cannot lead others until you lead yourself. Develop a practice of checking in on your own direction in life to stay on track.

TEN

IMPROVE YOUR EVERYDAY

'The only thing necessary for the triumph of evil is that good men should do nothing.'

Edmund Burke

The lessons in this book will certainly make your workday more enjoyable and help you to relate better to those that you work with. My wish for all of you who have read to this point is that you learn a few take-away lessons you can implement in your workday. I firmly believe that engagement in our work is possible. Find a job you enjoy and contribute to the vision, support others in your team and make a decision to remain more present in your daily interactions.

The greatest regret people have at the end of their life is wishing they had the courage to live the life they truly wanted. You can ensure you avoid this regret by calling out inappropriate behaviour, creating trust and belonging in all teams you are a part of and speaking your truth. Do not be a slave to a job that is not providing fulfilment; take one slow Sherpa step to more closely align your work with your values and improve your level of engagement every day.

YOU CAN MAKE A DIFFERENCE

'What you do makes a difference, and you have to decide what kind of difference you want to make.'

Jane Goodall

The feeling that you are making a difference to others in your every interaction is empowering and leads to greater life fulfill-ment. Who do you want to be? What impression do you want to make? Do you want to learn to act in a way more aligned to your values? The big question is, do you want to be happy and do you want to make the lives of those around you happier?

What is my contribution in life? I encourage you to answer that question. It might not be having a large mortgage, owning your own home or paying off a boat that stays at the marina because you are too busy working to get out on the water.

It might be showing kindness to your colleagues. It might be being the person who someone is willing to confide in at their darkest hour. It might be discovering the best version of yourself or being on a constant trajectory of self-improvement. It might be learning to play an instrument, giving money to charity, rescuing a dog or even writing a book! The art of living consciously everyday has more rewards than you can possibly imagine until you start slowing down and living at a slower pace. This is your one amazing life to do with whatever you please.

Live the life you dream of.

It is possible.

Start today.

Final lesson from a Sherpa

- To live like a Sherpa is to live more consciously in the present moment.
- To lead like a Sherpa is to put the needs of the collective ahead of the needs of the individual.
- To love like a Sherpa is to be loyal, honest and have full respect for the other party, while still having a difficult conversation if required.
- To work like a Sherpa is to remain focused, dedicated and engaged in the task.
- To be a Sherpa you are clear on your purpose, fully understand who you are, are aligned with your values and you are supporting others to reach their potential.

Anxiety is living in the future …

Depression is living in the past …

True joy and engagement with your life and work is remaining in the present …

Right now, in this very moment as you close this book, everything is okay. It's even more than okay, it is how it is meant to be, this is the universal truth … your next step is up to you.

ACKNOWLEDGEMENTS

Thank you to those who believed in this project and supported me in its success.

To everyone I have worked with over the years, you have all in your own way contributed to this work.

The 5am club – what an effort – thanks for waking up and co-writing with me to make this a reality.

To Christina Joy, Monique Richardson, Mark Butler, Shane Williams, Katie Rees, Sophie Kratz, Alan Hesketh, Isabella Alan, Joanne Flinn, Lisa Gerber, Colleen Creighton, Christine Yip – your support was essential and I could not have done it without you all!

To all of my advanced readers Zoë Routh, Glenn Azar, Alyssa Azar, Karen Graham, Kate Silverback, Karen Zalewski, Kim Shepherd, Arieta Gavriniotis, Kate Hill, Karin Eden, Bronwen Galpin and Kate Rowland – I appreciate the effort and feedback.

To my editor Michael Hanrahan and Anna Clemann from Publish Central thanks for walking through this process with me and all the guidance and belief.

To all my clients past, present and future, I thank you for trusting me to work with your teams and improve their fulfilment at work.

Jade Lee is a fan of travelling
and the great outdoors, she has been
from Antarctica to Iceland and much in
between. She confesses to being a bit all
or nothing in everything she does; not
only did she trek to Everest Base Camp
with her Sherpa, Gobinda…she married
him! Having experienced and witnessed
the best and worst treatment that a
workplace can provide, Jade is obsessed
with increasing employee fulfilment and
works with organisations to empower
teams to work better together. She
practises and instructs yoga, is passionate
about mindfulness, sustained mental
health and employee wellbeing.